FUTUREPROOF YOU

Grammar Factory Publishing
MacMillan Company Limited
25 Telegram Mews, 39th Floor, Suite 3906
Toronto, Ontario, Canada
M5V 3Z1

www.grammarfactory.com

Tomney, Kellie
        Futureproof You: 3 keys to reimagining your career and amplifying your impact in the new world of work.

ISBN (paperback) 978-1-989737-14-9
ISBN (eBook) 978-1-989737-15-6

1. BUS012000 Business & Economics / Careers / General. 2. BUS071000 Business & Economics / Leadership. 3. BUS085000 Business & Economics / Organizational Development.

Production Credits
Cover design by Designerbility
Interior layout design by Dania Zafar
Book production and editorial services by Grammar Factory Publishing

Disclaimer
The material in this publication is of the nature of general comment only and does not represent professional advice. It is not intended to provide specific guidance for particular circumstances, and it should not be relied on as the basis for any decision to take action or not take action on any matter which it covers. Readers should obtain professional advice where appropriate, before making any such decision. To the maximum extent permitted by law, the author and publisher disclaim all responsibility and liability to any person, arising directly or indirectly from any person taking or not taking action based on the information in this publication.

FUTUREPROOF YOU

3 KEYS TO REIMAGINING YOUR CAREER AND AMPLIFYING YOUR IMPACT IN THE NEW WORLD OF WORK

KELLIE TOMNEY

authentic fulfilled limitless.

ENDORSEMENTS

'Talented, career-driven people want agency and authenticity. They want to own the trajectory of their careers. In *Futureproof You*, Kellie has focused each of us to be the agents of change and custodians of our own working lives. **Taking charge of your future is a bold proposition, but truly must be the only way forward in what is sure to become known as the decade of disruption.**'

MATT CHURCH, FOUNDER OF THOUGHT LEADERS,
AUTHOR OF *RISE UP: AN EVOLUTION IN LEADERSHIP*

'Kellie brings warmth, enthusiasm, joy and excitement to her work. In *Futureproof You*, **Kellie's book takes you on journey from Reactive to Proactive and finally to Futureproof, supporting you to make your career dreams a reality.**'

MEGAN LARSEN, FOUNDER OF SODASHI SKINCARE,
AUTHOR OF *STARTUPS & SELF-CARE*

'In this thought-provoking book, Kellie Tomney argues passionately that you can take back your power, and take responsibility for managing your career and your life. **By unlocking her three keys and her evolving cycle of impact, you can realise your true potential, and make for a better world. There can be no more noble purpose.**'

GORDON CAIRNS, CHAIRMAN, WOOLWORTHS GROUP & ORIGIN ENERGY,
NON-EXECUTIVE DIRECTOR, WORLD EDUCATION AUSTRALIA

'Kellie is considered and inspiring. How heartening to have details of her own story shared to counsel others to pursue personal evolution for drive fulfillment. She has much to contribute to us all during these complex times. This book provokes reflection and provides tools that shed light for us all. *Futureproof You* is a must-read, particularly for influencers and leaders pursuing a path of positive impact in their careers and lives.'

KATHY HATZIS, CHIEF MARKETING & GROWTH OFFICER,
NON-EXECUTIVE DIRECTOR

'Kellie is a wealth of knowledge, an overflowing cup of compassion and a powerful True Believer with loads of belief, conviction and commitment when it comes to helping people, leaders and organisations not only navigate and maximise what's next but actually FUTUREPROOF. She's the real deal!'

CHRISTINA GUIDOTTI, SPEAKER, AUTHOR,
ADVISOR & THOUGHT LEADER

Contents

HOW TO USE
THIS BOOK

This book and its parts are big, bold and life-changing. While you will get maximum impact from reading the chapters in order, you can also flip open any page for daily inspiration. There are extra resources and inspiration on my website kellietomney.com also.

I've *purposefully* made space on the page and in this book for reflection.

I sense you may need and/or value space to reconnect:

with your dream,
and your aspirations for your career.

I know you need space to connect:

to the person inside you know can be more.

I've also purposefully removed thirty pages of statistics and studies (thanks to my very first reader and editor!). You know the new world and the Future of Work are here! You know the scale and pace of change we are dealing with. I don't want to create more panic. I want to create more proactivity and fulfillment (and joy – yes, it's possible!).

Instead, I've given you the global trends and opportunities and have discussed how to leverage them to amplify your career and impact. Actioning the Futureproofing Keys I present in this book does help! So, I've prioritised your precious time and energy in order to move you forward, rather than drowning you in data that changes daily.

Also know it's completely fine by me for you to think at any point, 'Okay, Kellie, I get it, I want it – can we fast-track this and do this together?' Just get in contact.

This book is designed to help you to get back in the driver's seat when it comes to your career, leadership, organisation and future. So, make sure you complete the Futureproofing Actions contained in each chapter, as these will help you do the real work and actualise the change!

I've included real client stories from various stages of the career adventure to give you an idea of the key challenges professionals are experiencing (you are not alone!) and to celebrate their progress and impact. Their names have been changed and their companies have been omitted for privacy reasons. They've done the Actions and are enjoying the new future they've created for themselves. You can too!

It's time, isn't it?

It's time to come back to your power. It's time to discover your next career, leadership role and life purpose, achieve your alignment and highest influence, and amplify your positive impact.

'WHEN YOU STEP INTO AND ACTIVATE YOUR PURPOSE AND BUILD YOUR BRAND

YOU CHANGE YOUR WORLD AND OURS.'

There are countless examples of my methodology Futureproofing people's careers, finances, wellbeing, relationships, leadership, organisations and lives. The ripple of purposeful positivity inspires, motivates and provides others with forward momentum and growth.

It's saved and futureproofed my life and livelihood and it can do the same for millions of others, including you.

Let's do this together. I can't wait!

K x

INTRODUCTION

Let me share a story from my past.

I'd always prided myself on proactively managing my career and taking roles that were in line with my values and that allowed me to grow and to make an impact. That's what made my role at the time so magical – I was helping other people do the same. I was leading a team who helped people find work in organisations where they could make their best impact in their career – a dream come true!

One year and one month later, however, things started to change.

The next major employer branding campaign my team and I had been working towards was shelved. The CEO, who was a major reason for me joining the organisation, announced her move to a competitor. Our new CEO, who had very different priorities, was announced.

Then... there was a merger / takeover.

Then... the big four consultancy firms came in.

Then... the cost cutting started.

Then... then... then ...

Then, we found ourselves having to justify our place in the organisation and fighting to show the value of what we had built, what we had poured our hearts, minds and souls into. What we'd worked for disintegrated. My role no longer existed.

I'd been so busy 'fixing' and 'firefighting' in order to overachieve in my current role that I had not prepared or positioned myself for the future.

The strategy turned from transformational, business-wide and global, limitless impact to cost-cutting and limited impact. I could now do my role in my sleep with capabilities I had in the first few years of my career, not the stretching, valuable ones that give me so much more satisfaction.

While we were in merger and transition mode, I was offered alternative roles. However, I felt none of them were aligned with my values or strengths or what drove me internally or what would make a big, meaningful impact. Work became like a pebble in my shoe. It wasn't the worst job (or life) but I wasn't being fulfilled or inspired.

Moment by moment, I could feel my purpose, value and impact was being eroded. Within every meeting and every presentation, I felt less engaged and less motivated. I felt myself getting smaller and smaller in terms of impact and value. I felt less heard; my voice was reduced to a whimper.

I began to question myself:

Am I satisfied that this is it? Is this all I have to give? Should I take the 'safe' roles offered to me or do I venture into the unknown to make more impact? Surely, I can contribute more than this? What's next?

On a deeper level, I thought, *Is this really who I am? Is this all I can be? I know I can BE MORE and make more impact.*

Before all of these changes, I had loved my career. I'd loved what I had achieved and the challenges it provided. I was senior, smart, educated, experienced, ambitious and driven. I'd become increasingly more influential, valuable, powerful and connected to my organisations and the bigger impact of my roles and what we could, and did, achieve. I truly loved getting up in the morning (yes, it is possible!). My mind was filled with ideas for improving things and my heart was filled with the connection I had with my team. I was purposefully motivated for the day ahead. I had always worked hard; I had consistently tried to better myself, constantly upskilling and trying harder. I got so much satisfaction from the impact we made.

But things outside of my control happened. Before the merger, I had been a corporate transformer and creator. After it, I felt like a corporate pretender. Pretending to be motivated. Pretending to be engaged. Pretending to be inspired to lead my team into the future. But pretending isn't in alignment with me. I had visions of me at the work desk being present but absent. What's more, these roles I was being offered weren't the impact that I wanted to make.

It was time to do some real soul-searching. It was time to make a change.

A big change.

I forced myself to confront my reality. My boyfriend of two years was in the US and the pressure had been on for one of us to move for a while. 'Just get here and I'll take care of the rest,' he told me and assured my friends.

Finally, worn down by my lack of Career Purpose and clarity, lack of a better path, and not being aligned with the impact I would be making in roles offered to me, I said no to other opportunities and I quit my job. I moved to the US to be with my boyfriend. I'd prioritise my relationship. I'd follow the call and the '1000 blazing suns of love that couldn't wait for me to get (t)here'. I'd figure out my next career move and life plan once I got there. At the time, I thought this was my best choice.

Right?

Wrong.

On my last day of work, I woke in the middle of the night with a sudden, then determined, instinct telling me to check my phone. That's when I saw it. The text from the man I was moving to the United States for.

That text instantly turned my career and life upside down. It contained four words no one ever wants to hear: *We need to talk.*

My stomach fell. My heart froze. My brain went into rapid fire: *What? You've got to be kidding? I'm moving countries for you. I've left my job, my team and my organisation. My flight is booked. The removalists are coming tomorrow. No, I have to be overreacting; this isn't what I think it is.*

I frantically left messages on a voicemail half a world away...

... and got no response.

I moved through my last day of work in a thick fog of shock. I smiled dimly at my team and all the people congratulating me on my romantic, fun, new adventure. All the while, I was wondering to myself, 'How did everything go so wrong?'

In the space of a day I went from:

- Earning a six-figure salary **to** having no salary.

- A comfortable house and lifestyle **to** no fixed address.

- 'Love of my life' **to** 'what just happened?'

- A 'life line' **to** complete free-fall.

- A proud Australian resident **to** an 'alien' with no visa in the US.

- Corporate career cover girl (literally on the cover of the annual report!) with a 'stellar, blue ribbon career' going according to plan **to** being totally career-less and unprepared for the future and what was next.

- Having made a unique, valuable, amplified, global impact **to** feeling diminished and worthless, zapped of confidence and of the contribution that I could make in the world.

All aspects of my life disintegrated.
I was unravelling: What next? What now?
What are my options from here?

While there was a lot I didn't know, there was something I was completely sure about.

As a senior executive woman, I had put my eggs into one basket – one organisation and one job that I loved – and it had changed overnight. Then I had put them into a relationship that I loved and that had changed overnight as well. In all the working so hard, caring, worrying and contributing to the organisation and my team, I had let others control my future. I had put the organisation and everyone else first. I hadn't planned options and I had been caught with the consequences of a 'work hard, give your best and commit – the opportunities and rewards will follow' career (and life) plan.

I was an award-winning executive who had built up global recognition of my expertise in maximising employer brands, leadership and organisations, and developing them for the future.

> *Yet, I had no future strategy or plan B for myself. Plan A had disintegrated into my mobile phone. I was so far from futureproofed, it wasn't funny!*

I was so far from everything that I would have advised anyone to have or be or do – individuals, leaders and organisations. I had been futureproofing others but not futureproofing myself.

It was time to get back in the driver's seat and to find a successful, sustainable and impactful path that was true to me.

I couldn't wait for my dream role and future to present itself. I needed to create it for myself.

A WORLD OF CHANGE

I share these experiences because I can relate to the constant internal call for career change as well as sudden, dramatic, out of your control, external catalysts for career change. I am well aware that millions globally and locally have it much worse than myself. And I see much more change coming and millions who are not prepared or positioned for it.

From my experience in this space over twenty-five-plus years, I'd say as few as two per cent of global workers have a future plan or career plan. That is why this book is so important!

After a tough journey back to clarity, I started a consulting business (during the GFC) from a laptop in a one-bedroom apartment in Washington DC – a city I had only known from a best-practice HR & Branding Conference and from the nightly news that beams around the world. I used my professional branding, change, recruitment and leadership skills to engage with clients around the world.

Over the next eleven years, that business would allow me to help thousands of executives, professionals, leaders and women to futureproof their careers, leadership, organisations and lives. I would help them to navigate the ever-changing external environment while remaining centred and aligned with their internal purpose, and amplifying their positive impact and contribution.

> *Futureproofing is my life's purpose – I don't want what happened to me to happen to you. I want you to create and maximise your future.*

Do a quick check-in.

Are any of the following statements true for you?

- I want a meaningful, impactful, fulfilling career.

- There is more to my career, leadership and life.

- I have more to give.

- I am overwhelmed with expectations, roles, workload and/or options and I can't see a clear path for what's best anymore.

- I don't have a career or future plan.

- I am not feeling my whole self at work.

- I don't want to sell myself or to be 'cut down'.

- I don't know how to brand myself authentically to be more influential, impactful and valuable.

- I don't want to regret not making the impact I could have.

- I am driven to achieve, contribute and be a role model.

- I have a need to maintain my livelihood and lifestyle (and others); I want to maximise my value, worth and impact.

- Something needs to change but I don't know what or how.

Yes? Then this book is for you.

You can BE MORE. You can MAKE MORE IMPACT IN YOUR CAREER. You can be your AUTHENTIC, WHOLE SELF and BE VALUED MORE FOR IT. You can ADAPT and MAXIMISE YOUR VALUE & FUTURE in an ever-changing world.

In Part 1, we will explore why you need to futureproof now. We will explore the state of today's new world, the major shifts and the common and constant career challenges, and our confusion about who we need to be and what happens if we make reactive choices.

We'll also look at the evolving expectations of employees and the Future of Work, and why we are crying out to make more impact in our careers. And we'll examine the increasing amount of career options and how that can make things even more confusing and complex. Finally, we will look at our addiction to 'overworking and underselling', and learning, fixing and bettering ourselves. In many cases, these hold us back and diffuse and diminish our impact.

In Part 2, you'll discover the 3 Futureproofing Keys and some practical ways to ensure you amplify the impact in your career by putting them into action. I'll be encouraging you to 'practise' these tools. Not because 'practice makes perfect', but because in using my methodology, I know that purposeful practice makes a bigger impact.

You'll understand that no one is perfect. No one. And what's more, it's more impactful if you aren't. Who you are is enough but, when actioned, these keys will unlock the impact you are craving to make. You'll connect to your best whole self (some for the first time in your careers and lives), your values, and discover your superpowers, your big aspirations and goals. You'll get clear on you, your potential and the future you want to create. You'll look forward to the future and you will plan aligned, agile options. You'll develop a unique brand and value that build your confidence and contribution. From this strong, stable foundation, you will take action with authenticity and alignment to amplify your positive impact. We will build your courage and you'll activate some of the highest value strategies that are proven to help make more impact in your career.

Finally, in Part 3, I'll illuminate that making more impact in your career is something that evolves. I'll share the pathways that we are all on. Through this, you'll see where you are at, no matter what career and life throws at you, *and* shine a light at the end of the tunnel. You are ever-growing and when you know the path, you can enjoy the adventure, adapt to new challenges and the new world, and amplify your impact along the way. By Refreshing, you'll continue to adapt and grow. You'll experience greater, amplified impact and you'll feel even more alive, fulfilled and valued.

I've been in your shoes and sat side by side with thousands of executives and professionals as they've stepped into their bigger impact. So, throughout this book, you will read about some of my clients and their experiences, impact and growth. These are real professional people in their careers, not celebrities and media personalities. The career and impact struggle is real and it applies to everyone. Their approachable stories will remind you that you are not alone. You'll start to see your value and impact skyrocket (or, as clients have said, 'the magic start happening').

After years of coaching and mentoring individuals and conducting hundreds of workshops, I've found one thing to be true…

… you can make more impact in your career, but you have to step into it.

These keys unlock the doors and using them opens up a whole world of more aligned, impactful opportunities when you continue to step forward.

But you have to step in. If you are waiting for someone to recognise your great work and contribution, and to come and pick you, you may be waiting all your career and life! The world and work continually change and you know the consequences are coming. Waiting won't work.

Your career and impact are far too important for that.

Are you ready to make that step?

Part 1:

WHY YOU NEED TO FUTUREPROOF

Constant Volatility, Uncertainty, Complexity, Ambiguity and Disruption in our world are making jobs, careers and industries more insecure.

The Future of Work and the fourth industrial revolution are here. Careers have changed and will continue to change rapidly and significantly.

THE QUESTION IS:

WILL YOU CHANGE WITH THE TIMES

OR WILL YOU BE FORCED TO CHANGE BECAUSE OF THEM?

WILL YOU LET THE FUTURE DICTATE YOU, OR WILL YOU DICTATE YOUR FUTURE?

In Part 1, we'll explore why you cannot wait for these consequences to reduce or limit your career, contribution, value and impact.

You need to futureproof your purpose and potential, and develop future-valued skills and a career plan with multiple career growth options. When you are clear, confident, prepared and protected, you can adapt, pivot, reset, reshape and reposition quickly in relation to change to BE even stronger, more fulfilled and more impactful than before.

Ready?

THE PROBLEM WITH BEING REACTIVE

Julia, a high performing, ambitious, self-confessed Type A career woman, was saying yes to everything. She was the major income earner, and she had what others would call a successful career to date, but she was driven internally and financially to progress her career and impact further. Something was missing...

She sat in front of me over coffee. I asked how I could help. She explained that she was doing everything. She was working her heart out. She wanted to give 110 per cent to so many things and deliver the best results; she was saying yes to everything and everyone else, and it was too much. On top of her director role, she was lecturing and marking at a university, had her side business, was writing a blog as a brand ambassador for a key brand... and the list went on. She really wanted to better her career and make a bigger impact. She had so many options for ways in which she could make a difference that she felt she was now not making much difference at all. She was lost and the only road she was going down was burn-out.

She was working so hard trying to fit in that she had lost herself and her confidence. She was senior in the banking and finance industry and would often be the only woman in the room. She felt she had to replicate what she saw around her to get ahead and that didn't feel authentic for her. She was splitting and changing herself for all the different roles in her life and she didn't feel she was doing any well. She had 'identity overwhelm' and it wasn't working. She wasn't feeling her whole self and even her colleagues were noticing her lack of confidence and that she was making less and less impact in all her roles. She was starting to feel invisible, even to herself. She wanted to be seen, heard and valued. She wanted to make an impact; it was at the heart and soul of who she was.

She knew something had to change. She would regret it if she didn't give her best in her career, having the skills and talents to make the difference that she knew deep down she could make.

She'd dreamed of achieving big things in her career but now her aspirations seemed distant and she doubted she could make her big career aspirations her career reality.

There were big changes happening in her organisation, industry and the world and she knew she would feel more fulfilled if she could make her mark. She wanted to find ways to get clear and to fill the hole that the lack of authenticity, achievement, stretch, satisfaction and growth was making in her life.

Her voice on important matters wasn't being heard; she was being judged, not seen. In truth, she was only using about twenty to fifty per cent of her potential, despite all the hours and stress and sacrifices she was making in her personal life for work. She wasn't branding herself; she 'hated that' but would see others less capable getting opportunities in areas she wanted to impact. She felt she was invisible to senior leadership and some external clients.

She was so busy fixing everything and caring for everybody inside her organisation and outside it. She was the 'go to' person but it was not getting her where she wanted to go – to the next level and the impact she so craved to contribute. She knew there was a better way to do things in her organisation and industry, but she couldn't get to it as she was overworked and overwhelmed while being undervalued and, truthfully, underutilised. (Can you relate?)

On the outside, it might look like you have it all – a good job, a good salary, a good house, good friends, good relationships, a good life – but deep down you're wondering, 'Is this it? I've got twenty to thirty years more in my career and I know I can make a bigger impact than this.'

A FUTURE PROBLEM...

First off, you are not alone!

I sit across the table or screen and speak to rooms full of executives and professionals every day who feel just the same.

And it's not your fault. The world and the world of work are changing, and that brings so many doubts and uncertainties with it, which can be paralysing!

You will be pleased to know I'm not going to go through pages of scary statistics. That would only serve to make you more fearful, highlighting the struggle ahead and spending our precious time on the problem rather than the proactive solutions.

What's more, you've heard all the statistics a thousand times before; you are bombarded with 'the robots are coming,' 'the current crisis is causing a decade ahead of more unemployment and underemployment, the deepest economic downturn since the Great Depression, largest budget deficits in seventy years, an economic recession and likely global depression.' The statistics and studies I include today will be out of date tomorrow, as they change daily and hourly. This is the scale and pace of change we are dealing with.

You already know the new world and the Future of Work are here and you can google statistics any time you like.

But what you don't know and you don't realise is... where the opportunities lie for you and how to leverage them.

There are global trends that you need to be aware of. In fact, there are eight key global trends that are influencing you and your career choices:

Massive global change:

We have big problems in many fundamental areas (economy, environment, social equity, health, education, politics, gender equality, careers, income and jobs) on a local and global scale. These issues are at critical levels, preventing our society from functioning effectively and optimally. Greater levels of global interconnectedness and interdependence mean an impact in one fundamental area across the globe literally affects us all in our careers and lives.

A yearning to make a difference:

A new age has commenced, moving from patriarchy and hierarchy to more partnership and empowered collaboration. There is an increasing trend towards more professionals and executives wanting to make a positive contribution and more impact in their careers.

Constant career insecurity:

High unemployment and underemployment are expected to continue for years to come. Continual change and disruption require you to plan and pivot, embrace change, and be more resilient, agile, adaptive and fluid, transforming more than ever before. You are truly in an ever-changing, unknown and emerging environment.

An old, outdated career system for a new world:

The 'job for life' has opened up to become 'many jobs for now'. There are so many more options for you to make an impact now (board roles, side businesses, your own business, freelancing and consulting, projects and collaborations, hybrid and portfolio career creation, to name a few). New-world free agents are thriving, while traditional, linear career and progression paths have been destroyed. The traditional career ladder has professionals stuck at all levels, especially those in the middle rungs trying to ascend and make a bigger impact.

An addiction to busy:

Overworking and over-stressing is not helping you achieve more. Firefighting and fixing and saying yes to everything and everyone are causing immense health issues in our workplaces and society. You can be so busy giving 110 per cent to your current role that you are not planning for what's next in your career. This leaves you more exposed to future-of-work impacts and working harder. This approach will leave you behind and making little lasting impact.

Generational diversity and increasing future-of-work complexity:

We have five different generations in the workplace all wanting to contribute. The workforce is more diverse and more complex than ever before. You have more flexibility in your career than ever before. It's more complex than ever to lead and make a difference as we have fast-forwarded to globalisation, artificial intelligence, virtual reality, digital technology, the internet of things (IOT), working from home, working from anywhere, and these all impact you and the new world of work.

Untapped potential left on the table:

Women are more educated, more career-oriented and more globally aware than ever before. So many have outgrown their current role; they can feel stuck and are capable of more in their career. They want to contribute more but there are pressures – both external (societal and social norms and systematic conditions) and internal (including negative self-talk such as: 'I don't want to brag,' 'I am not good enough,' 'I haven't done enough,') – that are holding them back from speaking up and being and contributing their authentic, most impactful selves in the workplace.

Online personal branding pressure:

Jobs in the new world are typically sourced by networks and online searches. You need to be known, continually adapting and valuable in the ever-changing future. If you don't learn how to authentically brand yourself, you will be commoditised, less sought after and left behind by others making a greater impact. Career women in particular 'hate' (a strong word, I know) branding and selling and talking about their achievements themselves. Professionals, business owners and leaders at all levels are expected to have a positive brand reputation and to be up to date and leveraging the latest in personal branding, social media and technology. It can leave many feeling 'old school', with an expiry date.

Ask yourself: Which trends are impacting you right now, and which ones will impact you in the future?

... BUT A BIG OPPORTUNITY

So, what to do?

Well, as the Buddhists say, 'Life is hard.' Irrespective of your spirituality, I think a few of us can agree with the sentiment here. We see and experience it all the time. Life is challenging. It is not easy. Managing your career and life is hard – especially given the trends above.

Your career (whichever pathway you choose) will not be all unicorns and roses and peace and light, but it does present itself with some real opportunities!

As professionals, we need to make the highest impact and add the highest value by futureproofing ourselves and our loved ones NOW, so we can have the highest level of enjoyment, satisfaction and fulfillment. You give a lot to your career and you deserve the rewards as well.

So, don't let the opportunities pass you by!

Acting on the following opportunities is your pathway to fulfillment.

OPPORTUNITY 1:
Prepare yourself for industry disruption and reimagine your career to get ahead

'My career path might not even exist. Industries are being disrupted. Profit and shareholder returns are harder to get. There is more restructuring, mass redundancies and disruptive change to come. Artificial intelligence, virtual reality and other trends are causing exponential shifts in the Future of Work. There is no job security, no stability and everyone is asked to do much more with less. White-collar and blue-collar workers are being replaced with 'new-collar' individuals. Constant career re-training is expected as well as the current 'day job' and learning is now expected to be lifelong, not a course or degree or two. What do I do?'

Sound familiar?

Whether it be a coronavirus crisis or global financial crisis, the year 2100 or 1920. The world is constantly changing. There will always be something outside of us that impacts our careers and lives. We can identify factors that are out of our control and prepare for them.

> *You can adapt, adjust and reset in order to keep moving forward and making your biggest impact.*

In March 2018's Australian Financial Review, IBM Chief Executive and Chairman Ginni Rometty alluded to the seismic shifts:

> *Something happens when both business and technology architecture change at the same time and you look back in time and it has the potential to change everything. If you can learn exponentially you become the disrupter, versus being disrupted.*

OPPORTUNITY 2:
Brand yourself and stand out authentically for greater impact

It's competitive at the top, mid and lower levels for jobs. There are fewer positions at the senior levels of an organisation and more people wanting those positions. Many people say they do the same work and have the same ideas, but they do not get recognised.

Hence, you can't sit back and wait to 'get picked'.

Authentic self-promotion is key –
and a huge opportunity for you.

OPPORTUNITY 3:
Build your online profile, presence and impact for the new world

The online environment, technology and expectations are changing rapidly and often, so we need to work out how best to tell our story to best position ourselves to achieve our goals. Think about those out-of-date profiles that you cringe at online.

Don't put this on your to-do-list for later, for when you have time (when is that going to be?).

There are high-value things you can do right now
to increase your profile, presence and impact.

OPPORTUNITY 4:
Take back control

Professionals want to reach great heights in their career and life. Some get to a stage where they feel their potential and value are not being realised. You can feel stuck, confused, frustrated and you want change. You want to do exciting things, but most don't know how.

Whether you are skilled and passionate, want more and have more to give, or you are driven to leave a legacy, you can take back control and proactively move forward.

I get that there are pressures and commitments and, often, a lifestyle that you want to maintain. There can be high levels of financial pressure and you can be highly committed financially with mortgages, school fees, expectations when it comes to holidays and lifestyle, and the list goes on. The thing is, the multiple pressures on your time and energy keep adding up and there is a different kind of 'cost'. That 'cost' can be less health, less fitness, less presence, less patience, less happiness... and less satisfaction.

You have to weigh up the cost of staying the same against the cost of opportunity. It's a short-term investment for a long-term gain.

OPPORTUNITY 5:
Create your Career Purpose to feel more fulfilled

Most professionals don't know their purpose in their careers. You can get lost over time, the more experiences and challenges you have. Remember Jerry Maguire and his predicament – he found he was clearer earlier in life than he was mid-life. It's not uncommon in career and life, where the answers aren't as clear as they used to be.

> *Creating your Career Purpose now will give you more meaning and fulfillment later.*

OPPORTUNITY 6:
Choose unique career combinations that maximise you

The days of one job being your one focus are gone. You can have multiple! How great is that?

There's part time, full time, flexi time, working from home, having your own business, having a side business, volunteering, freelancing, hybrid and portfolio career creation... and the options continue to grow for the new-world free agent. What may work for you today may be something you want to change tomorrow!

> *So, spend time working out your ideal career combination and maximise your potential. Then change the combination as you evolve.*

OPPORTUNITY 7:
Make a BIG difference to yourself and to others

Many crave career fulfillment. To be worthwhile. To be 'seen'. To be heard. To be understood. To be respected. To be valued. To make a real difference.

Yet, the cost of 'being strong', working harder and longer, and 'soldiering on' the current path is too high. Clients say to me, 'I want to make my biggest impact. I want to contribute and not regret I didn't do everything I could.' There is a way forward and light at the end of the tunnel.

You can do this!

OPPORTUNITY 8:
Elevate yourself to doing your highest value work

Doing repetitive, less meaningful work is not helping you or your career or anybody else (contrary to what you may let yourself believe). Doing these tasks and forgoing more important priorities is actually hurting you and your career. What's great is when you elevate yourself to addressing the more important and valuable priorities; you make more of an impact and because the work is more purposeful for you and you are more inspired and passionate about it, you shine!

What is even better is you don't need to be continually doing more hours (thank goodness, you say!) to get there. You can unlock the value of what already exists in you – what is crying out to be leveraged.

You need to step forward to prepare, position and authentically promote yourself and your impact now, so you are ready for whatever the future throws at you.

This is your opportunity to become futureproof. Don't leave it too late. It's time to get ahead, which is exactly what we will do next.

KEY POINTS

Continuing to work harder is not the answer or cure!

◆

Unless you change, nothing will change.

◆

You need to own and drive your career and future.

◆

You are more than good enough! But you need more people to know it.

◆

You are going to have to step in and get better at bringing your value to make a bigger impact in our new world.

◆

You can authentically brand yourself, your value and your impact.

◆

We need your best, biggest impact to create our best, new world.

◆

Getting out of the passenger seat is needed more now than ever before.

◆

You need to create and activate your future-valued and adaptive career and future plan NOW. Don't wait to be caught with consequences.

◆

Take the opportunities NOW.

ACT NOW!

I was having an online session with my client Debra. We started working together when she was Director of Strategy & Development. The company saw more potential in her and that she could make more impact than she currently was.

She had started her career in banking and finance and had been at her current organisation for a few years. Her career strategy so far had been 'head down, do the work and you'll end up in a good place.' I asked her how that was going for her and she said, 'It's not. It's not stretching or satisfying.' How insidious a lack of impact can be.

I asked what she wanted from her career and then the driver came... 'I want to make BIG IMPACT. I want to max my impact. I want to make a big, satisfying contribution. I want to be bigger, broader and more influential. I want executive roles and board roles.'

Like so many of us, she identified she was spending too much time doing lower value work versus addressing the higher value, BIG priorities that she was capable of.

It was confining and diminishing her impact rather than amplifying and expanding it, and it was eating away at her.

Since focusing on impact, her career and contribution have started to change quickly. She is productive (as opposed to busy!) working on important things but, in her own words, now she is clear on her purpose, and the impact and contribution she wants to make. She wants to have a career where she sets the agenda for companies, helping them drive significant change. She wants to be an evolutionary leader. She has stepped into broader strategy and her authentic, valuable brand. Three months down the line she has been promoted to Managing Director and she is now increasing her impact even further across other industries in her same organisation.

She has amplified her career and impact, and that was only possible by taking steps in the right direction.

> *What do you need to do now to help you maximise the opportunities that are available to you?*

FROM FRUSTRATED TO **FUTUREPROOF**

Belinda is a CEO who wanted to plan and prepare for 'what's next'. She didn't know what it looked like. She just knew she had reached a limit in her current role and she wanted to contribute more and move to the next level.

We discovered that her current brand was centred around being: Young, Talented and Smart. And when we developed her vision for her future, we realised that her current brand wasn't going to get her there. It was authentic but misaligned with her next-level vision. So, we updated and stretched her brand. Her Futureproof Personal Brand elements were: Strategic, Commercial Growth and High Impact Leader. Her unique Career Purpose was: 'To be and create the platform, and facilitate the vision and pathway, so that we plan, invest, activate and prosper in a shared, strong, more optimistic future for generations to come.' We used her future vision to focus and motivate her towards aligning with her future. What's more, she felt challenged again, adding the next level of skills and purpose to her career and life. From this, she targeted which study she wanted to do (she went from 'I'll have to do an MBA' to choosing specific financial study, which added more value to her future at less cost and in less time).

She stepped up to her next level. She broadened her impact across the country. She was receiving spontaneous feedback about how authentic she was, how in her truth she was, how much stronger she was becoming. She stretched her brand and her future to her next-level contribution.

> *Your next-level contribution is there for you to stretch into too!*

Some proactively plan for 'what's next'. With workforce changes worldwide, there are more restructurings and redundancies than in previous decades. It is affecting all levels of the workforce. Organisations are continually reviewing, resetting, redefining and reshaping, rebalancing and evolving their workforce requirements. Unemployment and underemployment are impacting millions worldwide.

> *Many are affected by restructure, reduced hours, redundancy or being stood down before they have pre-planned and positioned themselves for 'what's next' in their career.*

Ian contacted me on LinkedIn. He had been made redundant and, as a result, he was in the process of assessing what was next for him.

I actually knew Ian from a previous corporate role. From this, I knew he was high performing and on the company's talent list at that time. He was a director of high calibre and, like so many others experience, he was in the wrong place at the wrong time.

He had been given outplacement support and he had been utilising that for over a year. He did his best to give me his pitch and to seem as positive as he could. He explained that he had met with over 200 people for 'coffees' over the year. He was exhausted. He didn't know how to keep up the energy, how to keep fresh and how to make the impact he longed to make back in the workforce.

He had left it too long to strategically and purposefully act. The actions he had taken had drained him and decreased his value in the market. He felt abandoned and his employment options were decreasing. The long search was stressful and having an impact on his family, health and outlook on life. He said he was feeling like he was using only ten per cent of his potential and he wanted a new approach for this new world of work. His future and livelihood depended on it!

Unfortunately, he chose to continue with the same provider and the same outplacement approach that got him to this point – to 'save' investing in coaching. I have to say it – an 'old-world' outplacement approach. This approach is not fit for the way careers and the world have changed. Who wants eighteen months (and counting) of 200 coffee meetings with no work? In contrast, the payback of the new-world approach to careers can come in months. Think of the cost of even a year not working financially, let alone the other costs (increased stress, pressure on relationships, health and self-worth, loss of his impact in the world).

That's not what I want for you. This new-world approach has a far greater success rate! What it may cost to rethink your career will pay off for years to come.

> *Since careers are getting more complex and are changing so significantly, you need help to grow into the next stage of your career, and that starts by identifying where you're currently at, and where you need to get to.*

GROW WITH YOUR FUTURE

I've found that we experience the following impact and growth stages in our careers (Figure 1). As you read through each description, see if you can identify where you're currently at.

FEELING	POTENTIAL ACTIVATION	BRAND, PLAN, SKILLS, VALUE	IMPACT	GROWTH OPTIONS
FUTUREPROOF	120%+	++++	Amplifed & Ever-growing	Abundant & Growing
Stand Out	100%	+++	Transformed	Many fulfilling
Activated	80%	++	Accelerated	Influencing more
Unlocked	60%	+	Elevated	Directing
Frustrated	40%	–	Confined	Where next?
Disconnected	20%	– – –	Diminished	Few, if any
Abandoned	0	– – – –	Destroyed	Decreasing

© Kellie Tomney

Figure 1.

Abandoned/Disconnected

This is where you feel like you are going backwards, spinning your wheels or going in circles in your career. This can feel like you are at a career dead end. It can feel like you are in a black tunnel and you don't know your way out.

The potential inside you is being wasted; your brand, your skills value and impact are being diminished or destroyed by increasing external changes and disruptions. You don't have a career and/or future plan and your impact and growth options are decreasing. You feel disempowered and uninspired in your career and life.

You can feel your health and wellbeing are suffering and you can sense that you need to do things differently urgently, for your sake and for those around you. You can experience exhaustion, difficulty sleeping, overwhelm and not eating properly, and you may be overworking or under-working, where you start caring less and have little balance in life.

You don't feel you've got structure that is supporting you. You don't 'feel yourself', and you may not feel as if you are on solid footing within yourself and in other relationships. You can feel as though you are not being 'seen', 'heard' and/or 'valued'. You can feel really alone, and some may be depressed at this stage.

> *You can feel rudderless, lost and purposeless.*

Frustrated

If you are in 'neutral' and feeling demotivated, then you can feel frustrated and stuck. You can feel as if your energy is being zapped. Your potential is not being realised. You can be counting down the days in the week, starting to resent the business and role you are in. Many in this position feel unfulfilled, blocked and powerless.

At this stage, you can feel your brand is undervalued and your impact is confined. You can start to feel small. There is much you want to say and impact but, commonly, factors such as an old patriarchal system affecting the board and leadership level and organisational structures that can't keep up with external change may be holding you back. You may want to influence more effectively but, potentially, you are not feeling heard. You may not be a values, strategy or stage-of-organisation match. You may not be invited to key meetings that you want to be in, and others may be getting opportunities that you really want. You typically haven't, and hate, branding yourself and haven't made time to network.

You start to worry (maybe for the first time) about your ability to maintain and secure your lifestyle and livelihood. Often the main income earner or a major contributor, you don't know where to go next, but you know you need to do something to ensure you are positioned for the future. At the same time, you can be overwhelmed with workload and leading through crisis and/or continual change. Often, you are a person helping the organisation reset, recover and reshape but are not strategically helping yourself.

You may feel starved of the 'how to' and answers. You often go to networking events in the hope of finding a way to be more impactful and influential. While you can get inspired by affirmations and stories of high flyers, you can feel even more alone, leaving without any practical guide tailored for your own career environment.

You can feel alone and like there is no one who has been there, who sits where you sit, trying to apply theories and affirmations in a corporate career, leadership and business context. The fears of 'I am not good enough,' 'I don't know enough,' 'I am not enough,' 'I need to do more,' can be very loud at this stage. Typically, you may feel additional study or more qualifications will fill the gap.

Deep down, you long to amplify your career and impact and you know something needs to change.

Unlocked

In the Unlocked stage, you can feel like you are doing some of the work you enjoy in the career you like. You have more clarity on your brand, your career and future plan, and your valued skills. You feel more elevated and have more direction and are making progress. You have days in the week where you are making more impact and are feeling more valued, and others where you aren't as much. The low-value noise doesn't take you off course as much.

> *Your clarity has started to build confidence and you are being of higher impact.*

Your yearning to be seen, heard and valued starts to be fulfilled. You are speaking up more, sharing your viewpoints and solutions. You are feeling less invisible to colleagues and senior leadership and key external contacts. Your inner power is unlocked, and energy and impact start to grow.

At this stage, your results and impact haven't been maximised.

Activated

In the Activated stage, you are making progress. Your time is being utilised on more high-value priorities and more of your potential is being utilised, but you know you can do better. You have your authentic, valued brand, you are activating it (you feel relieved that you've got over those branding limitations), and your career and future plan empowers you to move forward. The clarity and increasing confidence have unlocked some more courage to step in, speak up more and take on more interesting tasks / roles / projects / meetings / responsibilities / leadership / opportunities. Your impact and value are accelerated and you are influencing more. It feels good!

You are starting to feel energised, authentic and aligned in your role and career path.

The results are flowing and are giving you energy. You are saying no to the lowest impact and lowest value actions. You keep saying yes to the highest value and impact priorities. It empowers you and you are making more impact. You are actioning new beliefs, stepping through your fears and you are moving into current and future alignment.

Your Personal Brand is visible and is giving you great energy, also energising those around you. Your confidence is turning to more conviction in your role, your broader influence and your ability to expand into new areas. Others are noticing a difference in you and it's contagious. Progress, success and positive impact are accelerated. You know you are enough – inside and out. You know there are always challenges but you have your core brand and future plan and, for the majority, you can stay centred and agile in making your highest impact contribution.

Stand Out

You have been authentic in your branding, aligned in your activation, focused on highest value priorities and it's all increasing your contribution. Your belief in yourself and your biggest career dreams is cemented. You've built your internal belief – you know you are more than good enough. You've understood the limits that hold us back and continued to step through them. You've grown more powerful and impactful. Feeling more authentic and uniquely valuable and on purpose fuels you on even further. You feel empowered and inspired to create and expand an even better future for others. You are well positioned with multiple career options and you are an active leader in creating a better future in the areas important to you. You are feeling whole, worthwhile and worthy. You are BEING more. You actually have more time to be more impactful in the areas you've chosen. Your contribution is powerful and influential and your impact is amplifying and expanding.

If you are at the STAND OUT stage, this is when you are recognised as a STAND OUT in your business and maybe others, and opportunities (projects you've wanted to be on or lead, new roles created for you, a new career portfolio combination) and new solutions are coming to you.

Your brand is known; your impact is transforming things. The difference you are making is so fulfilling that you are attracting even more fulfilling options to yourself.

You are known; you have proven experience, expertise and value. Premiums can be charged, and you get to work with the organisations, people and/or clients you choose, on the high-value, impact projects and initiatives that are most satisfying for you. Generally, people are attracted to you in career and life, and people want to work and socialise with you. Often, impact can be at an industry or national level.

Futureproof

This is where you are loving your work and career and it's sustainable and impactful in the new world and on your terms! You are feeling that real sense of career accomplishment. The burden of unrealised career dreams is history. You have a sense of worth, purpose and freedom that you know is solid and futureproofed.

Your joy in your work is reflected in your overall happiness and the results are there with great financial rewards and lifestyle. You have defined what success is for you and you're relishing it.

Your potential is being actualised, you are seeing great results and you feel and are experiencing your limitless potential. You are thriving in today and in what you've got planned next. You have many new opportunities and growth falls into easily alignment.

You feel clear, authentic and confident. Your brand is authentic, powerful and valuable and you are making the contribution you were born to make. You are ground-breaking in your career and impact. The days of ground-hog day in your career are so far behind you and you know you will continue amplifying your impact and thrive on ever-growing to new levels.

You are standing IN and owning your power. You feel aligned inside and out. You are influential and are making positive impact wherever you go. You are highly valued currently and into the future and have options that you flex and adapt to as the market and the future evolve. Regardless of economic recession, depression, recovery, rebuild, boom, bust, prosperity or peak, you are flexible, futureproofed and fulfilled.

You are so much more valuable. Career options are more abundant and growing. You are setting the course for your career and future. You have had pay rises, more responsibility, different and more interesting tasks/roles, more fulfilling connections, more influence, and the benefits have transcended your career. You know you are good enough, you actively step into and create more impact, and you're inspiring and a role model to others. You are leading and living a new, better career and future.

Here are some examples of what my clients say FUTUREPROOF & BIG IMPACT means for them:

- Creating the platform and pathway to prosper in a shared, more optimistic future for generations to come.

- Being an inspired, trusted role model who leads through critical and complex structures so that businesses and lives thrive through change with greater value and impact.

- Being in my ideal corporate role, feeling at my best.

- Accomplishing what my soul came here to do.

- Being creative, collaborative and contributing and enjoying to my maximum in career and life.

- Authentic in my career and life.

- Feeling my whole self and transforming results.

- Having achieved my long-term career goal.

- Being on boards in the areas I want to make a difference in.

- Loving my current role and giving back to the community.

- Having successfully moved from my corporate role and being in my successful business.

- Managing my corporate role and my side project for my financial future.

- Living my Career Purpose.

- On track to partner, having my business's full support, my wellness business outlet as well, and enjoying my life with my husband and new baby on the way.

FUTUREPROOFING MEANS YOU AMPLIFY YOUR CAREER AND POSITIVE HIGH IMPACT AND VALUE IN THE AREAS IMPORTANT TO YOU!

YOU HAVE MANY FULFILLING AND INSPIRING OPTIONS.

You activate your purpose and potential and positive impact when and how you want, with whom you want. This may mean CEO roles, board roles, C-Suite roles, starting your own business, mentoring, volunteering, painting, learning languages, surfing, starting your own charity, investing in businesses you care about, being there for children or caring, always speaking your truth in all your relationships, doing everything aligned with your values.... whatever you choose to maximise your impact. New connections, opportunities and transformations are available to you – often on a global scale here.

Where are you at?

So, where do you sit? Be honest now – there's no judgement.

A career fulfillment survey diagnostic – my survey results of ambitious career professionals hungry to make an impact in their career – indicated that:

- Thirty-one per cent of professionals were at the Frustrated stage / confined impact;
- Sixty per cent were at Unlocked / elevated impact; and
- Only nine per cent were between Activated and Futureproof / accelerated to amplified impact.

The important thing is you step in and we move you forward and up the stages in your career and impact!

The good news is that you *can* make more impact and you *can* be growing more significantly. I'm not about asking you to do more. I'm asking you to be focused on delivering the highest impact and the highest value priorities – **to be more**.

Here are some examples of the change I've seen happen with clients:

Sarah went from being a manager who had started to feel 'small and unheard', with no clarity in what she wanted to do next and with no visible corporate role models to 'being an inspiring, trusted role model, leading through critical complexity so that businesses and lives thrive through change with greater value and impact'. She is now a director on the partner track with multiple fulfilling career options.

Tim was a 'successful consultant but wanted something more and to make a difference to the matters that mattered most to him'. He is now a leader for Community Change and a spokesperson and advocate.

Jo went from being told she was 'too young and needing more experience to be on boards' to being on two boards. She is Deputy Chair for Industry Advisory and COO, while managing family and life.

Kylie went from being told she 'needs to work more time in locations in a similar role before she progresses' to being an award-winning HR director in another firm and a key executive leader taking business from $450M to over $1BN in three years, while raising a young family.

Anna went from being a HR manager to running her own successful consulting business in her passion area – empowering women in leadership and pay equality, while nurturing flexibility for her family.

Naomi established her own successful consulting business in three months in her passion. She built her own business and income, while having the flexibility she desired for her family and life.

Michael went from feeling frustration, exhaustion and despair, not being able to see the way forward and his way out, to being the most inspired he has ever felt! He feels like he has 'wind in his sails' and he is so clear and empowered for his next steps. He is going to start his own business while working in his current role, transitioning with the safety net, building up for further future changes.

> *We can all CHOOSE to be impactful leaders of our own careers and lives – so CHOOSE to change!*

BE MORE

Remember, your career doesn't have to continue along the same old path, with the same old routines.

Your comfort zone is comfortable, but nothing grows there and nothing of high impact and value lives there, so changing will be uncomfortable at first.

There are so many stories in history and in everyday life where people overcome seemingly unsurmountable obstacles, sometimes even life-threatening, and they go on to create a life where they feel futureproof, high value and high impact. They create a new world for themselves and others.

In reality, most of us are privileged to have been educated and we are not threatened by massive, debilitating obstacles as much as others experience in their careers and lives. Yet, it's quite common for me to hear: 'I can't do that,' 'I wouldn't get that role,' 'I have to focus on the (insert business / team / clients / kids / partner / parents / house renovations… anything else right now so I don't step into this),' 'I can't change or impact that.' I compassionately call out the fears that keep you small.

You can be futureproofing and creating positive impact today, but you do have to work at it. Inside and out.

Ready?

KEY POINTS

Know where you are at in your career
now and where you need to get to.

◆

Choose to make your BIGGEST IMPACT.

◆

You are as futureproofed as the impact you make. If you
make little or no impact, you and your career will be
commoditised. You are one competing with millions. If you
create current and future value, and make a unique impact,
you will be sought after forever. You will impact millions.

UNLOCKING
OPPORTUNITIES

Gabrielle is a leader in the Fintech space. She has won multiple awards and has been recognised as a key thought leader in her emerging industry. Her career is very important to her, however, at one point, she felt that she'd hit a career ceiling in her corporate role. She said she was using just two per cent of her potential before we started working together. It was dire! She was making limited impact and she knew she had more to give in her career. This was also impacting her health, relationships and life.

She stepped in. She witnessed the fears holding her back and she stepped through them. She started to make far greater impact inside her organisation and out. She attracted new opportunities that were aligned to the future career and life she wanted to create.

Actioning her new, diversified and expanded career and future plan cemented her personal brand in the industry at a new level and inspired her to think and impact bigger. And it paid off.

She is now an advisor to start-ups, building her network globally, completing an international masters and setting up a collaborative business in a creative field that she wants to help prosper. In the meantime, she has moved to a country that is a better fit for her and her family.

She is happy to report that she is now utilising 120 per cent of her potential. In the last nine months, her impact has amplified exponentially. She has transformed in her purpose, potential and impact (career and life). She has unlocked multiple opportunities for her to make the difference she was born to make.

Are you ready to do that too?

HAVE YOU EVER HAD A FEELING
THERE'S MORE TO YOU
THAN THE PERSON EVERYBODY
ELSE SEES
A PERSON HIDDEN DEEP WITHIN
THE VERY FABRIC OF YOUR SOUL –
YOU MUST PULL THAT THREAD
UNRAVEL THE TRUTH OF YOU
AND WAKE WITHIN YOURSELF

**THAT GREAT GIANT
YOU ALREADY
KNOW YOU CAN BE.**

– ATTICUS

Part 2:

THE FUTUREPROOFING KEYS

Now you know why you need to identify opportunities that amplify your career and impact, let's explore how you do that.

There are three Futureproofing Keys to your success, as shown in Figure 2.

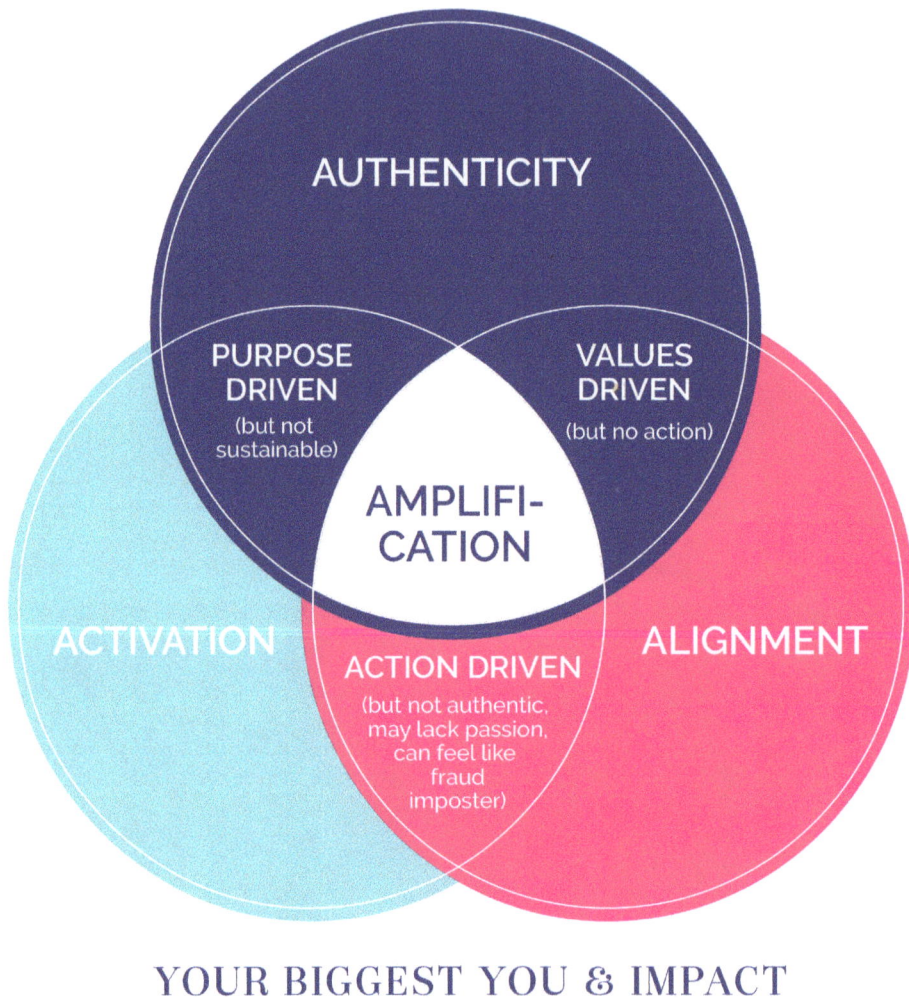

YOUR BIGGEST YOU & IMPACT

Figure 2: Your 3 Futureproofing Keys

© Kellie Tomney

Authenticity

Being yourself and bringing your whole self to work can be much harder than it sounds. We unlock your best you and your personal brand so you can be yourself authentically and be true to your values in increasingly challenging and changing times.

Alignment

You want to make a big difference in your career and world. Here, we create your Career Purpose and match your unique superpowers with what is valued in the market and world, now and in the future. We develop multiple future career options for you in alignment with your vision and goals and ensure your personal brand is in alignment and valuable in the future, so you can adapt as, and when, the world changes.

Activation

We get you into your power zone and focused on the highest value and highest impact priorities to amplify your impact. When you step in and activate these priorities, you are far more impactful, influential, adaptive, growing and valuable.

THE COMBINATION OF THESE THREE KEYS UNLOCKS AMPLIFICATION.

AUTHENTICITY + ALIGNMENT + ACTIVATION = AMPLIFICATION OF YOUR IMPACT

It's like binoculars – until you get the combination right, you can't see clearly. Once you have that combination for you, you can see miles into the distance, further than you ever imagined and it's magnified.

Clarity, confidence, courage and contribution are all amplified and the person is fulfilling their purpose, potential and making a bigger, more amplified impact.

I have seen this thousands of times. When people unlock the combination to being authentic, in alignment with the future and the future they want to create, and strategically activating the highest value actions, they amplify their impact X10.

What's more, its more effortless. It just flows. Opportunities come to them. It's that perfect pitch that you can hear for miles. It's a joy to see, hear and to be around. These people are in their power zone; they are doing what they were born to do and be. They are loving their work and life. The impact amplifies and attracts purposeful career and contribution opportunities.

So, let's do this!

KEY 1
AUTHENTICITY

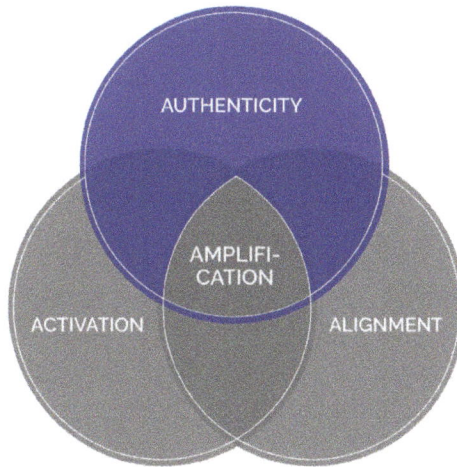

After reaching a significant personal and professional change cliff and it upending my career and life, I decided to go to Washington DC in 2009. With the little rationale I had left, I felt I had to go – I felt I had nothing else. My identity was shattered and my future plans, well, they were unknown. It had all evaporated before my eyes What was I to do? Why had this happened after I'd said no to other jobs and options?

So, I got on that plane and left behind my 'old' world. I had no job, no visa, no house, no income, no purpose and no plan. I moved through the days on limited capacity. I went from place to place and meeting to meeting, and I followed lead after lead, trying to make my story and life mean something again. I asked myself: Who am I now? Who am I *really*? What is my identity? What am I to do now?

What is my authentic self?

I knew what I *had* been: a senior corporate executive and leader living in Sydney with great friends and family.

I went deep. Under the pressure, state of urgency and lack of career and financial security, I dialled up my Career Purpose- and soul-searching. I read books, sought out coaching, went on more personal and professional development courses, went on retreats, visited healers and clairvoyants, meditated, worked out and upped my various yoga and master classes hoping *to discover who I truly was*.

So, like with an onion, I peeled back the layers to discover who and what was at my core. This was a painful, confronting, career- and life-threatening, mind- and all-consuming process. There wasn't a moment I wasn't thinking about this stuff because I knew it was the key to my survival – literally!

I re-evaluated my values, my strengths, my passions, my purpose, my why, and what I really felt was true for myself. I did all this work and needed to bring it into something practical and purposeful. I needed to create an anchor for myself. The seas at this time were very rough and I felt I was being pulled in many directions.

This is what it means to be your authentic self. To be yourself amongst changes and in all conditions. To this day, I get feedback on how authentic and resilient I am. It remains in my brand and keeps me anchored through ongoing change. *I can keep my core and adapt authentically.* Authenticity is one of my superpowers and one of my most valuable ones.

After thousands of presentations, the consistent theme I get back from people is: 'I loved your authenticity and your stories. You are true to you inside and out. It makes me feel as if I can do this too.' And you can.

I know I am true to myself. I accept my whole self. I know who I am (with and without my work), what I stand for, what value I add, the unique impact that I want to amplify and the options for where I am going.

> *Authenticity involves being rooted in your deepest purpose, beliefs, values and truth and living a life that is a true reflection of them.*

DON'T FAKE IT TILL YOU MAKE IT

'Know thyself.'
– PLATO

'To thine own self be true.'
– SHAKESPEARE

'Be yourself, everyone else is already taken.'
– OSCAR WILDE

We crave authenticity. We want authenticity in ourselves, others, leaders and organisations. It's so valuable that people connect with it and are attracted to it.

We sense if a person is not authentic. We can spot a fake a mile away. It devalues everything they do and say and who they are. (Do you really follow and give your best to an inauthentic leader?)

When you feel authentic, you feel whole, and your energy and influence are more powerful.

Authenticity allows you to unlock your unique value.

If you are not authentic, you won't attract aligned, high-value opportunities to you. Because you are unclear on who you are and who you want to be, your impact is fragmented and diffused. Inconsistency distracts from your highest value.

Why are brands like Coca-Cola and Oprah so impactful and valuable? They are authentic. They know what they stand for and they consistently activate it in everything they do.

Authenticity is your core. It allows you to stand in, stand out and stand up. In reality, the majority of executives and professionals in our careers do not know or show their authentic self.

You are unique; you have authentic superpowers, and we need them.

We need you to own your authenticity so you can align and activate it for highest impact.

To do that, you first need to identify what your STANDOUT ADVantage is.

YOUR STANDOUT ADVANTAGE

Your STANDOUT ADVantage is made up of three things:

- Authentic superpowers

- Differentiators

- Values

Let's explore each in detail.

Your Authentic Superpowers

'Live in your strength.'
– LAO TZU

Most of us go through life without knowing our superpowers or even our strengths. I see client after client who draws a blank when I ask them to list their strengths. This hurts me at a soul level. It's a crying shame. If we don't even know our strengths, how can we fully leverage them for positive impact in the world?

I've been a long-time follower of Oprah. In an appearance in Sydney entitled *How to turn up the volume in your life*, she spoke about finding the common thread throughout your life to be able to maximise your life. I know that's easier said than done, so we are going to discover your common threads below – if we pull these together, we can see what your authentic superpowers are.

FUTUREPROOFING ACTIONS

When have you been at your best in all areas of life? (It doesn't matter when it was. It could have been high school, while travelling or doing community work, or in a recent program at work). Let's capture it. There is always a superpower element that we are going to capture.

- What was the situation?

- What were you doing?

- How did it feel?

- Who were you with?

- Why did it feel like you were at your best?

Why do you need to know your superpowers? When we pull these authentic super-powers together, these are things we're going to highlight in your life. It gives us a clear guide to what your best authentic self looks like.

So, looking at your answers, what do you notice?

If you are stuck, here are some examples of superpowers to help: Intuition, Innova-tion, Insight, Instigation, Independent thinking, Influencing ability, Ideation, Inclusive approach, Inquiring ability, Improving Processes, Incisive decision making, Inquisi-tiveness, Inviting change, Implementation, Imagination, Inspiring leadership (these are just some starting with I) .

See also if you can recognise superpowers in the client stories presented in this book. You might spot ambition, drive, kindness, compassion, empathy, natural leadership or vision, for example – and find you resonate with some of these qualities yourself.

The list is endless, and the combination will be unique to you.

> *Now you know what your superpowers are, we're going to look at what makes you different.*

Your Differentiators

A client was recently explaining that she felt an interview had gone poorly. She had been authentic in her truth, admitting that the role might not be a fit for her as she didn't have government experience and explaining she really wanted to be in an environment where she could make changes. She had also been upfront with the fact that she is a mum and she wanted to work flexible hours where practical. Well, it turns out those three differentiators got her the job. That's exactly what the company wanted. It wanted outside experience. It wanted a shake-up to make real change, and its mission was to work flexibly and showcase how the company could work in the future.

The rewards are there for those who are authentic and do stand out, but it's comfortable and perceived as safer not to stand out. Fears arise. Tall poppy syndrome and imposter syndrome can cut us down and make our impact smaller, when we think, 'It's better if I try and fit in.' The 'fitting in' strategy essentially gets you nowhere as you don't show your uniqueness and full value; you are not bringing your best to the situation and, what's worse, you feel small and you get further away from the amplified career and life that you could have.

FUTUREPROOFING ACTIONS

Reflect on the following questions:

- What makes you different (inside and outside of work)?

- What do you do and have that others don't? What are you that others aren't? (Unique skills, work and personal experiences, intelligence, expertise, viewpoints and values that others don't have can actually became a differentiated advantage for you.)

- What story can only you tell?

Your Values

In our increasingly complex world, it's more important than ever to know what you stand for.

Nikki, for example, was a senior manager aspiring to become a director. In addition to her corporate role, she had a side business. Everything was looking great, but she revealed that, honestly, she was overwhelmed with the state of the world, industry change and her work reshaping, and in this state she wasn't going to big contribution to any one in particular.

We centred in on discovering her authentic power values for her at this time in her life. While she cared about many things, the clarity on what she really, really, really cared about reduced all the clutter and mind chatter.

In a nutshell, for her, it was important to be a role model in the finance industry; she stood for financial independence, for women in particular, and wellness. What was valued by her organisation and others, and what they said would add more value to her, was her being a leading role model showing that it can be done, bringing her unique client network and contacts to the firm, and being more clear and confident in her communication. In their words: 'Be more in your truth versus comparing to others.'

So, while it was both confirming and a little hard to hear, we were very clear on what Nikki's best authentic self was – when she was clear, confident and unapologetically true. Others valued her speaking up more and contributing more, not so much the late nights doing 'fixing' work.

The clarity allowed her to power up her impact and contribution. Now, Nikki has elevated her career; she has been promoted a number of times since and she is a now becoming a sought-after speaker in her industry, becoming a role model for new leadership, wealth and wellness for those in her world.

So, that's what we're going to do for you.

FUTUREPROOFING ACTIONS

Reflect on the following questions:

- What are your authentic power values? What do you really, really, really care about? (Sadly, most people don't know their values. If you want some help, go to my resources at: www.kellietomney.com)

- What do others value about you?

- What do others say would add more value to you?

- What do you want to be known for?

YOUR FUTUREPROOF PERSONAL BRAND

Now you know what your superpowers are, how you're different and what your power values are, you are on your way to creating a futureproof brand. But what do we mean by that?

Jeff Bezos is renowned for saying, 'It is what people say about you when you are not in the room.'

In the world of social media, globalisation of work and the internet of things, personal branding has been on the rise. I chose to study marketing and HR at university and have always been fascinated by the intersection of people, brands and business and how it can be optimised for organisations and careers. Initially, people thought of personal branding as what they were wearing. While image does have some impact, there is so much more.

We know just how important it is to know your personal brand and to market and position yourself for the now and new future opportunities.

YOUR PERSONAL BRAND IS THE TOTAL EXPERIENCE OF YOU.

Sure, the business suit, the business card and the collateral matter, but no one of those is the standout. For businesses and products, we know branding is valuable. Personal brands are rising in their impact and value. Oprah's personal brand is worth far more than that of some organisations.

> *You are a brand. Right here, right now.*

Whomever you have met / worked with / emailed / spoken to today has formed a view of you. Everyone who has ever met you has a filing cabinet with your name on it. It only takes seven seconds in person and two seconds online for someone to form a personal branding impression:

- It is people's total experience of you.
- It is how people describe you.
- It is your reputation.
- It is how people introduce you to others.
- It is what they say about you when you are not in the room.
- It is the experience they have had and expect to have with you.
- It is the size and strength of your network.
- It is the unique value you contribute to a company, your social circle and your community.
- It is *every* interaction with you.

And more...

... it builds over time and it is defined by others' perception of you – good, bad or otherwise.

Does anyone think you can wave a wand and just change your reputation and the total experience others have with you? Not with a wand, but with authentic self-awareness and then purposeful activation – you can.

CONCENTRATE ON YOUR INNER REALITY FIRST.

FUTUREPROOF YOU

KELLIETOMNEY.COM

We've all seen the Instagram affirmations ad nauseam: 'Be you' and 'Be yourself, everyone else is already taken.' I believe there is positive intent in these, but I know, personally and professionally, that it is easier said than done. It's easier to preach this than to practise it.

It's difficult to truly be ourselves. To unearth shiny diamonds and gems, we must sift through dirt. To create a brilliant painting, we must use shades of dark and light. It can be a lifelong journey to become truly authentic and aware and to embrace the different shades of you that will help you shine for your greatest impact and value. Standout individuals know what they stand for. Critically, they stand for it under pressure. What I stand for has been tested and has evolved over time, and I expect it is the same for you.

At the heart of it is your personal brand essence: your truth. Surrounding that are your brand personality and values. There is a lot to it, but, essentially, you can condense your standout personal brand to unearth your unique attributes, strengths, skills, values and passions and use them to attract opportunities to you.

Every day, I run workshops and speak to and mentor people one on one who want to amplify their career and impact. They want to make a greater contribution. They want to make the greatest impact they can make and to be valued for it. They want to stretch themselves to achieve their highest potential. They want to be authentic but they also want to stretch. There is an art and a science to this, and I've worked on it over time. It's the unique combination of your Authentic, Differentiated and Valued (remember, your ADVantage) self that will achieve your future superpowered career goals.

My ADV Personal Brand has changed over time to help me achieve my goals. If I had taken a snapshot of my personal brand at times in my career, it would have looked as followed:

- Positive, nice and effective (Yes, Kellie is 'so nice'. While it was authentic at the time, this personal brand wasn't helping me progress my career or make the most impact, value and contribution I could make! I consciously stretched my personal brand to 'strong' and it's helped amplify my impact and value ever since.)

- Positive, resilient, purposeful

- Purposeful, strong, successful

- Authentic, purposeful, successful

- Authentic, superpowered, limitless

- Authentic, fulfilled, limitless

These have huge significance, meaning and purpose to me. They guide and stretch me through difficult days and times, and the dream days and times. You need to find your unique combination to stretch you.

YOUR SUPERPOWERED FUTUREPROOF PERSONAL BRAND

IS THE MOST EFFECTIVE WAY TO CLARIFY AND COMMUNICATE WHAT MAKES YOU DIFFERENT, SPECIAL AND VALUABLE TO EMPLOYERS, CUSTOMERS AND THE WIDER COMMUNITY, NOW AND IN THE FUTURE.

FUTUREPROOFING ACTIONS

Reflect on the following questions:

- What is your current personal brand? No editing... what would people really say about you when you are not in the room?! When it comes to the roles and career options that you want, what words and statements come to mind?

- What do you want it to be? Write a list of words that capture who you want to be and what you want to be known for. (We will build on this in the next chapter: Alignment)

- Pick the three most impactful words from your Authentic superpowers, Differentiators and Values for your SUPERPOWERED FUTUREPROOF PERSONAL BRAND

VALUE AND BE VALUED

Being authentic is a great step, but when it's not valued by the market or externally, that's when it's career and soul destroying – believe me! That's why we need the Superpowered Futureproof Personal Brand combination **and** the next two Future-proofing Keys, ensuring you're Future Aligned and Activating your brand authentically in the highest value ways.

Once you are living authentically, your confidence will start to soar, and you'll start to step into a bigger game. You'll be much more comfortable stepping into branding for bigger impact, as it's authentic to you!

Then you are ready to align yourself with your future – that's what we will do next!

'TO BE OURSELVES CAUSES US TO BE EXILED BY MANY OTHERS AND YET TO COMPLY WITH WHAT OTHERS WANT CAUSES US TO BE EXILED FROM OURSELVES.'

— CLARISSA PINKOLA ESTES, PH.D, WOMEN WHO RUN WITH THE WOLVES

KEY POINTS

Don't fake it till you make it or try to be anyone else.

◆

Focus on you being your BEST YOU.

◆

Know your STANDOUT ADVantage:

Your Authentic superpowers

Your Differentiators

Your Values

◆

Uncover what your personal brand actually is – what it is currently and what you want it to be. This clarity gives you authentic confidence.

◆

Be clear on who you really are at this stage of your career and life.

STRETCHING AUTHENTICALLY

Kathryn contacted me after an online presentation. She, like almost all of the attendees, said she was unsure what her personal brand actually was – to herself and to others – but she knew it was holding her back in her career. In our work together, we captured the many authentic, favourable superpowers she had. Her confidence was building... she felt good. She could now own these 100 per cent.

We explored what others would think and say her personal brand was. That's when her voice dropped and she got quiet. Gently, we discovered that her personal brand to others was along the lines of: 'a great doer', 'go-to fixer', 'loyal', 'a giver', 'overworked', 'reliable', 'committed', 'stuck in the day-to-day'.

Her career aspirations centred around leadership. Impactful leadership. Her current brand was not going to get her there. She agreed – it was time to take charge. We stretched her into her Superpowered Futureproof Personal Brand: 'confident transformation leader', 'strategic high impact', and 'broad and adaptive'.

While it was a stretch, it was based on her authentic superpowers and her desire to be more in her career. She started to shine. She was bringing and adding her insights in meetings, her intelligence was getting noticed and she was building key relationships for the organisation and for her future. She was getting feedback on how much more commercial and confident she was.

Her business went through a major restructure and she was one of the few that kept their job and got a better, broader role that presented her with new skills in a new area. She is now looking forward to the new world and has a pep in her step to be doing something new, saying, 'I now feel fulfilled and in the right direction. Totally different to six months ago.' Thankfully, also, this gives her better career and financial positioning for her future, an especially big relief being a single mum.

What part of yourself are you holding back that you need to step into?

KEY 2
ALIGNMENT

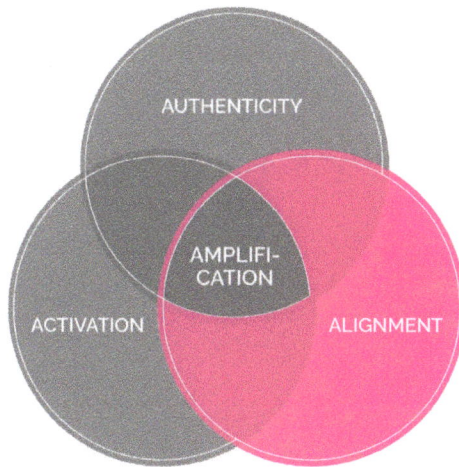

Stephanie achieved most people's
version of success at forty-something.
And herein lay the problem!

She didn't know what came next. When it came to her next phase of career, she had 'no idea'. One thing she did know was that her current workplace was not in alignment with her values.

She was a partner in a law firm. She was recognised in business, she was on an economic development board and she had a government board role too. Externally she was successful, but internally she felt hollow.

She was acting on auto-pilot and because she was highly competent, she could do that, but she felt highly demotivated. Circumstances meant she had no voice in leadership matters. She had become really disengaged with who she was and what she wanted. When she sat in a workshop with me, she realised she had achieved a lot of the things people were stating as goals but she didn't have an answer to what she wanted to do next and who she wanted to be in five years' time.

We worked on creating her 'what's next' future vision and options to achieve her more fulfilling future. We created her Career Purpose for this next stage and the steps to align with her future vision.

Two years later and Stephanie is practising law at a whole new level. She is activating her (now clear) future vision with her cofounder. Their fresh, engaging purpose is actioned every day – enriching clients, enriching community, enriching employees – and they have abandoned old habits, replacing them with clear, communicated, future-aligned approaches.

Her personal brand, values and Career Purpose have become core again; she's recognising it in her choices, and actually making choices not just about WHAT she does, but with self-awareness around WHY, HOW and with WHOM, which is critical. She's aligned in her values and with a future that is valued by the market and herself.

> *This is what happens when you're in alignment – you put yourself in a position where you amplify your current and future value.*

Alignment became key for her personally and in her leadership, and we had future-proofing sessions with her co-founder and business team.

The benefits are internal and external. She feels authentic and engaged inside and out, and her business thrived during and post the coronavirus pandemic as their flexible, tech-savvy and enriching values had already been put in effect in the business' future-planning.

Stephanie is authentic and connected with the future she wanted and created and is prospering in her Career Purpose, aligned with the work she loves, how she loves to work and whom she works with. If she had stayed in her previous role, her value would have decreased and her impact would have diminished.

Her business has expanded and reaches clients locally, regionally and nationally, even amidst a global and local crisis – that's futureproofing!

> *Future Alignment involves being clear on your career and future plan, and your Career Purpose, having multiple options to adapt to changes, and continually developing, expanding current and future-valued skills and energy.*

YOU WILL GET THE FUTURE YOU ALIGN YOURSELF WITH

We know the new world is here and we have to expect more change. So, to future-proof ourselves and our careers, and preserve our livelihoods, we must reset and align with the new world of work.

In reality, most of our workforce is aligned with an outdated job or career and that is no good for them, their organisations or society. We have big problems that can be solved by people like you, who align with the now and the future. As Warren Buffet said, *'There is no use running if you are on the wrong road.'*

Many are approaching career dead-ends, road-bends and cross-roads, with restructuring, redundancies and reskilling ahead for the workforce of the fourth industrial revolution, Industry 4.0. You have a choice to align with the future or not. You will get what you align yourself with. It's up to you!

I'd love you to choose a present and future filled with fulfilling, rewarding, career- and future-abundant, growing options rather than stale, old, unfulfilling, energy-sapping, limited options.

Most executives and professionals are so busy on the treadmill that they don't know where they want to go.

> *When you are clear on your authenticity and your future alignment, you can be it, attract it and amplify your energy and efforts.*

When you align yourself with your biggest, best self, career and life, and when you're authentic, and present and future-aligned, you make your most powerful impact.

'YOUR FUTURE DEPENDS ON WHAT YOU DO TODAY.'

– MAHATMA GHANDI

You can't just expect a great job or career to come to you. It's increasingly competitive – there are more people for fewer roles. You have to maximise your value. Old skills will become automated. Artificial intelligence, big data, augmented/virtual reality, the digital age – they are all here today. You can't expect to keep your job and make a big impact by staying the same. You'll be outsourced or overlooked. I realise this is tough to hear, but it's true, and it's tougher if you don't do anything about it. I want to futureproof you. To do this, you need to Future Align and Activate. Be the future. Be your future-aligned brand. Be your biggest impact.

Have I motivated you yet? Let's get going on Future Alignment for you.

> *You get what you focus on, so we are going to focus on your purpose, your authentic self and elevating your brand.*

'GO CONFIDENTLY IN THE DIRECTION OF YOUR DREAMS. LIVE THE LIFE YOU HAVE IMAGINED.'

– HENRY DAVID THOREAU

WHAT IS YOUR LIMITLESS VISION & GOAL CAST?

I was presenting and a woman came up to me afterwards. She was almost crying, as she had had quite a breakthrough – she told me she had realised she was living her family's version and vision of success, not her own. She was an accountant and she decided then and there she was going to envision and plan her career (and life) change.

In another workshop, a participant came to the realisation that, over his career, he had just kept taking the roles offered to him. Another role was being offered to him and he wasn't going to take it because he didn't love it. He recognised he had pre-viously fallen for the flattery of being offered these roles, but once he had taken them, they had left him flat, uninspired and not maximising his career or impact. They were adding to the organisation's vision and future plan, but not to his.

FUTUREPROOFING ACTIONS

Grab some paper and on one page, create your LIMITLESS VISION & GOAL CAST. This is your future limitless plan. I recommend it have all your key areas of life on it (career, financial, health, wealth, relationships, personal growth, physical environment, community, spiritual, emotional, self-care). Consider:

- What future goals and aspirations do you have?

- What does your future vision look like if you have no limits? (Expand on this for all areas of your life and ensure it includes all the elements of your best YOU).

- What does it look like in five years' time?

This ensures you create a future that lights you up from the inside out!

Next, we will define your Career Purpose so we can use your superpowers to fuel your future vision and get there faster and with less friction.

YOUR CAREER PURPOSE

A client's business was bought by a private equity firm and a new CEO appointed. It was challenging for the whole business and her division in particular. We had created her Career Purpose and it gave her the confidence, courage and conviction to take her stand amongst huge change. She knew what was consistent and motivating and what would be most successful for her team, the organisation and society. That's what a Career Purpose can do!

Her team knew it was authentic to her; they remained as engaged as they could, maximising their performance and contribution in tough and challenging times.

Consistently aligned with the future she wanted to create, she put her purpose into action despite the challenges, telling her team: 'The new owners may be different to you and me, and perhaps to our agenda. We both want to beat the competition and most importantly we want to keep production in Australia, serving Australians, and keeping Australian jobs. We can only do this if our Australian based businesses are globally competitive and that is what we need to continuously strive for – that is our responsibility and our obligation to ourselves, our families and the broader Australian community. What a privilege! Let's reinvigorate and re-engage with our mandate and our KPIs – leveraging and developing suppliers that are globally innovative, optimally costed, and sustainably focused for a better Australia and a better world. Together we will look after each other; together we will deliver. Stay strong, stay positive, believe in what we do.'

'**FINDING AND LIVING IN ALIGNMENT** WITH THE INNER PURPOSE IS THE FOUNDATION FOR FULFILLING YOUR OUTER PURPOSE. IT IS THE BASIS OF TRUE SUCCESS.'

– ECKHART TOLLE

It's easy over time to think you are only what you do, but it's who you are and the WHY that are critical and that make the long-term impact.

Her team will never forget her Career Purpose or her brand.

What will you be remembered for?

Early on in my business, my purpose was to 'help companies become a great place to work'. I fully believe if we have more engaged employees, we have higher performance, higher profits for good and we make a much better impact on the planet.

Over time, I added more about focus on the individual. Why? Because I believe in the unique superpowers of individuals and the impact all individuals can make.

We have 7.7 billion people on this planet and if we have people standing out authentically and aligned in their careers, and able to make the most impact... imagine the potential being harnessed and realised!

Helping individuals achieve their ultimate Career Purpose and potential is still at the core of my purpose today.

Your purpose is the unique gift you bring to the world.

It defines who you are in all contexts (as a leader, executive, business owner, aunty, mother, father, friend, etc.)

It's your personal North Star, something you use as a reference point to guide you through life and keep you on the right path.

Your purpose should be something you are relentless about, that you constantly wish for, think about, worry about, obsess about... it probably keeps you awake at

WHAT WILL YOU BE REMEMBERED FOR?

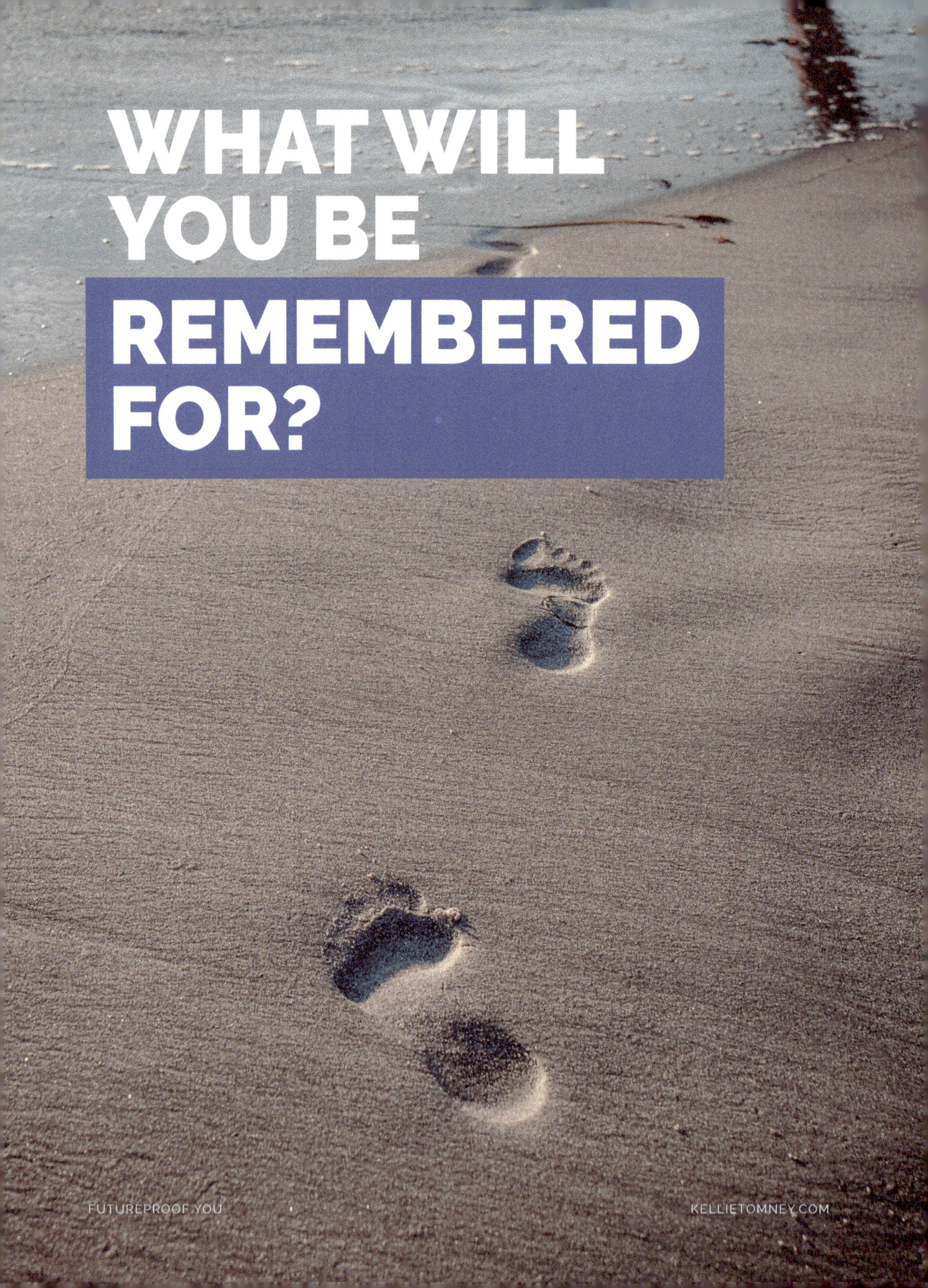

night with concern. Have you got something or some themes that come to mind? Now we are getting closer.

When your intention comes from your highest purpose, it powers your actions and results. Your purpose is to share your gifts (or unique ADV superpowers) and to live aligned with your values.

Your purpose is within you. You have to do the work to discover it and unblock it to be in alignment and flow.

KNOWING YOUR PURPOSE GIVES MEANING, JOY AND DIRECTION TO YOUR LIFE.

KNOWING YOUR PURPOSE GIVES YOU POWER.

FUTUREPROOFING ACTIONS

Reflect on the following questions:

- Describe some moments – in work and life – when you have been most proud.

- What was the specific contribution you made to the lives of others during these moments?

- What impact did you have? What did this moment allow others to **do** or **be**?

- By reflecting on these answers, get to a sentence about your purpose that inspires you and has value in the future!

'S/HE WHO HAS A WHY TO LIVE FOR CAN BEAR ALMOST ANY HOW.'

—FRIEDRICH NIETZSCHE

YOUR FUTURE CAREER PLAN...

How much time do you spend planning your holidays? How much time do you spend planning your career?

Research shows that we spend ten times more time per year planning a car purchase than our careers. We spend 1.5 hours an entire year on career planning and twenty-two hours a year planning a holiday! (Workforce 2020 skills, Dr. Tracey Wilen-Daugenti, Apollo Research Institute)

A car and a holiday are depreciating assets. You lose money on a car as soon as you drive it out of the show room or pick it up from the owner. And on a holiday as soon as you get home, when you can dread going back to work.

No wonder we are not maximising our careers and living our potential. We are investing in short-term, quick fixes. We are not investing in the career that drives us financially and purposefully.

Your career impacts your life and your life impacts your career.

IBM CEO Ginni Dimmity has said that 100 per cent of roles are going to change. Even if you're in the same role, you're going to have to re-design your career for the future. I agree.

> *Our careers are appreciating assets;*
> *maximising them makes us money and*
> *gives us fulfillment in life. Our careers are*
> *most worthy of investment.*

Now, some say you can't future-plan your career because 'life is so unpredictable,' 'the future is unknown.' I call BS on not being able to future-plan! If you genuinely want something in your life, you don't wait for it. I'll show you how to factor in the emerging, changing future and the unknown.

So, now we have your Limitless Vision & Goal Cast and we have your Career Purpose, we are going to create multiple career options for you to achieve it all! We have started with the end in mind – the future you want – and now we will develop the career options aligned with your purpose.

Having multiple options means you can adapt when things change. As they frequently do!

... WITH MULTIPLE CAREER OPTIONS

So often, we defer to government, politicians, organisations or our hierarchical leaders to futureproof our careers. Yes, they play a key role in this, but *you* have the leading role in your career and your life.

Having multiple options empowers you. It helps futureproof you. Every day, I speak with people who haven't futureproofed their career. They feel stuck and fenced in. Their basic freedoms are jeopardised. They feel they need to stay where they are financially and/or emotionally; it eats away at their confidence, their life and the contribution they could be making in the world. In the majority of cases, my client here is a woman. She will say, 'I have to stay where I am because of the children, my husband, my partner, my parents, my mortgage, etc.' Many women say, 'I don't have money of my own,' although they would have been earning money for decades as career women.

While this sacrifice seems noble and selfless, it is in fact selfish. It denies us the best of the person; it denies us their full contribution. So, to get real here... I want all of us to have multiple career options. This means you!

Not having a career plan and continually being on the treadmill with little control doesn't help anyone.

As Simon Sinek says, in *The Infinite Game*, *'One of the most powerful things we can give people at work is discretion. What you find is that the more control people have over their careers, it not only breeds more engagement and innovation, but it actually reduces stress.'*

I agree and I've seen it at work for twenty-five-plus years. Minimal options or one option confines you.

Take John, who had been in the same industry, same organisation, same/similar role for a number of years. He could foresee the role wasn't going to exist in the future; he felt it would affect not only his career but his relationship and life. He wanted to work for many more years (he was only in his early forties) and didn't know his 'what's next' career options. If unattended, he knew his bouts of stress and dissatisfaction in his job and career could lead to depression. He planned to maximise his roles in the industry *and* his transition to new industries to futureproof his career and options.

We have more career options now than we have had in previous decades. I call it the 'paradox of choice': part time, full time, work from home, board roles, hybrid and portfolio career creation, working at a community level, global level, local level, etc. Although I would never want to take away the increased options now, it does make it harder to choose. This can be a career conundrum for many. I've had clients who have wanted to do everything, from being head of a division to running a non-profit to becoming a counsellor to teaching yoga.

By now, you will be familiar with the 'hyphenated' professional identity and portfolio career where people leverage a combination of multiple careers at once. For example: the marketing-director-swimming-coaching-business, lawyer-board-member-traveller-caregiver or the finance-leader-mother-artist.

We are going to cover this in more detail. For now, there are no limits or filters and you can choose later. Let's look at your multiple options.

Note what can happen here is that you revert back to your comfort-zone thinking...

and the career you've always been in. But the stats say that only fifteen per cent of employees are engaged in their jobs (Gallup), so I see you. Let's not limit what could be the most fulfilling and most impactful career options for you. Put all options down and we can refine later.

FUTUREPROOFING ACTIONS

Reflect on the following questions:

- Building on your Limitless Vision & Goal Cast, now go limitless in your five-year career options. Think specific roles, companies, industries, countries, global and local. Add all that come to mind.

- Think various portfolio combinations also (e.g. two part-time roles and your own business which you develop over time) and add them too.

- What options do you have outside your current organisation? Your current industry? Your current job? Your current work structure (full time, part time, volunteer, board, etc.)? Ensure you have contingency options and have planned for different scenarios.

- What are seven options for your career that allow you to fulfill and contribute your career purpose?

By adding a number of options and planning for scenarios such as jobs and careers outside your organisation and outside your industry, it ensures you are more futureproofed and forward-planned and not caught by surprise when, let's say, a coronavirus pandemic occurs and your current job is made redundant. You've foreseen a circumstance where you may need to change organisations or industry and you've pre-planned and pre-positioned yourself for smoother adaption and change.

So, now we have your Limitless Vision & Goal Cast, your Career Purpose, and your Multiple Options Career, you can flex as the future evolves!

'FAILING TO PLAN IS PLANNING TO FAIL.'

– BENJAMIN FRANKLIN

BE VALUED BY THE WORLD

We are in the new world. Your career choices are either to be controlled or to be free and fluid and flexible in the Future of Work.

I recommend keeping up to date with future-valued skills, industries and the jobs of the future, and activating high-impact and high-value priorities towards that future. Often, it will mean adding projects, new skills, courses, study or seeking out mentorship to your career plan and, of course, actioning it (more of this in the next chapter: Activation). Your job and livelihood do depend on it.

We need to be proactively and continually preparing ourselves. We are facing the greatest employment challenges since the Great Depression. Millions globally are out of work, and old skills and old career mindsets are not going to be valued in the new world we find ourselves in.

Ten skills for the future workplace, as identified by the Future Work Skills 2020 Report by the Institute for the Future, are:

1. **Sense making** – the ability to determine the deeper meaning or significance of what is being expressed;

2. **Social intelligence** – the ability to connect to others in a deep and direct way, to sense and stimulate reactions and desired interactions;

3. **Novel and adaptive thinking** – proficiency at thinking and coming up with solutions and responses beyond that which is rote or rule-based;

4. **Cross cultural competency** – the ability to operate in different cultural settings;

5. **Computational thinking** – the ability to translate vast amounts of data into abstract concepts and to understand data-based reasoning;

6. **New media literacy** – the ability to critically assess and develop content that uses new media forms, and to leverage these media for persuasive communication;

7. **Transdisciplinarity** – literacy in and the ability to understand concepts across multiple disciplines;

8. **Design mindset** – the ability to represent and develop tasks and work processes for desired outcomes;

9. **Cognitive load management** – the ability to discriminate and filter information for importance, and to understand how to maximise cognitive functioning using a variety of tools and techniques;

10. **Virtual collaboration** – the ability to work productively, drive engagement, and demonstrate presence as a member of a virtual team.

It's fair to say we've seen the importance and need for these skills already, let alone further into the future. With some of these skills, it is difficult to even understand the definitions, let alone for most of our current workforce to practise and be leaders in them. But we must all keep learning.

Other future-valued skills include: embracing change, adaptability, innovation, vulnerability, bravery, courage, creativity, new leadership, resilience, reinvention, and overcoming hardship and challenges.

> *Consistently adding future-valued skills and solutions to your Futureproof Personal Brand will insure your career and livelihood.*

In addition to future value-adding skills, you need to align towards helping solve some of the biggest problems in our new world. Your contribution may be in improving our environment, energy, our economy, our equality, our education, peace and justice, politics, social equity, our health, technology, innovation, our networks, our leadership, our communities or our companies for a better, new world.

My dream is for every person to have a unique, positive, valued contribution to a better future. I want us to be proud of who we are, what we are becoming and what future generations will inherit from us. My methodology is purposeful and practical when it comes to increasing people's clarity, confidence, courage, contribution and consciousness in order to create a better world through their careers and their amplified positive impact.

A common attribute of my clients is that they want their purpose and profits to be for the greater good and for a regenerative system and planet. By activating their unique purpose, their work and their income for the future (or effectively transitioning to it), people contribute to the collective positive growth of humankind.

YOUR FUTUREPROOF PERSONAL BRAND & FUTURE-VALUED SKILLS

Now you have created your Limitless Vision & Goal Cast and Multiple Options Career, let's think again about what brand you need to achieve it. We need to ensure your personal brand is aligned with and valued in the future, and we need to stretch you into living this 'best you' brand.

FUTUREPROOFING ACTIONS

Reflect on the following questions:

- Imagine your future dream role has come up. The bosses and recruiting managers have the applications in front of them and they are talking about yours. What would they say?

- Pick five people you need to influence to make the decision regarding your application (your boss, your boss's boss, key team members, a boss in another division, HR). What would they say about your application? Write down three words/comments from each person. No editing – we want real insights here.

- Imagine the next level of leadership – what would they say about you as a person, professional and/or leader when you are not in the room?

- What future-valued skills do you need to add to your career plan?

- What contributions to current and future problems and solutions can you add to your career plan?

- What does your FUTUREPROOF PERSONAL BRAND need to be now? It's likely that it has stretched further and that there is a gap between your current brand and your Futureproof Personal Brand. What is the gap?

POSITIVE IMPACT

My moments of connection with my clients post the 2020 coronavirus lockdown guided my refreshed inspiration and purpose. Everyone has families and friends who are suffering and without work and income, but they are futureproofed and are not freaking out. They feel as settled and strategic as you can be throughout this. They are stepping into their authentic power and are getting new levels of respect and rewards. They are shining, leading lights for a new, positive, ever-growing way. They are the ones getting the new positions in the restructured, reshaped world (one of the options we had planned for) and they are feeling as clear and confident as they can be. They have broader, multiple career options. They are leading themselves and others through the complexity, change, chaos and crisis to a better world. They are not wishing for the past, to go back to the 'old normal'; they are leading and living the new way and their career and life purpose. And this is what gives me mine: 'To inspire and amplify strategic, positive impact so that we create and live a new, better future.'

Now you are clear on Future Alignment for you, you know you can't just visualise it and have it happen, don't you? I wish... but, in truth, we have to activate it and step into being it.

You have your unique roadmap for your present and future. So, let's go. This is where we put your authenticity and your future-valued vision into action!

'THE PURPOSE OF LIFE IS NOT TO BE HAPPY. IT IS TO BE USEFUL, TO BE HONORABLE, TO BE COMPASSIONATE, TO HAVE IT MAKE SOME DIFFERENCE THAT YOU HAVE LIVED AND LIVED WELL.'

— RALPH WALDO EMERSON

KEY POINTS

Most people don't have a career or future plan.

◆

You get the future you focus on and we want you to have the best career!

◆

Create a Career Purpose that brings your unique
superpowers and contribution to the world.

◆

Create your Limitless Vision & Goal Cast to give you direction.

◆

Develop your Multiple Options Career to be prepared
and best positioned to adapt and be flexible in the face
of expected, constant and emergent change.

◆

Consistently adding future-valued skills and solutions to
your skillset and stepping into your Futureproof Personal
Brand will insure your career and livelihood.

◆

Authenticity and Alignment give you clarity and confidence
and now you need Activation to make it a reality!

ALIGNING WITH YOUR FUTURE

A client was referred to me, as she wanted to work through 'what's next?' career-wise. Michelle had a corporate career in the media and entertainment industry and had had years out of the workforce caring for her young children. In her heart, she didn't want to return to the 'corporate world'. I coached and mentored her through the 'Futureproof You' framework and we went limitless in our thinking and Futureproofing in our strategic planning! She started her own consulting business as a business strategist for small business owners and was quickly working with whom she wanted to work with and making a sustainable income and living. Having her own income, financial security and independence became even more valuable to her as she suddenly became a single mum.

Being future-aligned with the market and the future she wants for her life, she has given herself added career options. She is more futureproofed. If she needs to pivot to another option, she can. If she hadn't done this work, she might be back in a job and career that doesn't inspire and engage her, nor maximises her career purpose and superpowers! Instead, she is now connected with a thriving, inspiring, additional network, she's built her personal brand and her business brand, and she's increased her value and financial base for the future.

What future will you align with?

KEY 3
ACTIVATION

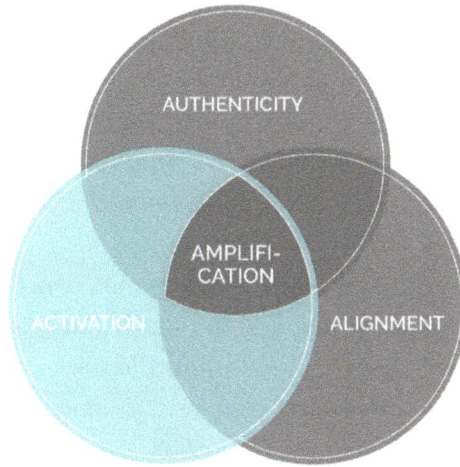

I met with Jo after a presentation I gave. I could sense how accomplished she was without her saying a word. Do you ever get that? But when I asked her how she was going and feeling in her career, it didn't match up.

She said she was not clear; she was muddled. She knew what her strengths were and was authentic in herself. She thought that others would see her as 'hard working', 'a quick thinker', 'intelligent', 'analytical' and 'empathetic', but she revealed she (like most of us!) lacked confidence.

Internally, she was driven to be an achiever for good in her career. Externally, she was a quiet (almost silent) achiever, not an overt achiever. When we talked through some examples of what that meant for her, we saw it meant that she undersold herself to her peers and her boss. She didn't network. She had been asked to speak at industry conferences and she had declined. Only the people she worked with closely (i.e. her team) knew what she was capable of.

She was an extremely effective general manager in a crucial industry. She had MBA, BBA, CPA and AICD qualifications and over twenty years' experience in finance and accounting. She had demonstrated success in maximising business performance. She had been part of 5X growth outcomes. She had her team behind her and other functions actively seeking her out for new solutions. She felt authentic in herself and she had an idea of the future career she wanted, but she was not activating it.

She was not maximising her intelligence, her energy and her efforts consistently every day. She was not actually making her best and biggest impact in her career. She was being small, and it was affecting and limiting her. We started working together before the coronavirus pandemic and, during that, her husband lost his previously very secure job through no fault of his own. While her lack of career activation had been affecting her and limiting her career previously, it was now weighing even more heavily on her loved ones and livelihood.

She gave herself one out of ten for Activation. It's more common than you think. What would you give yourself for Activation in your career?

Do you know people who talk about what they want to do, what they are going to do, and/or why they can't do it? We can all fall into this at times. Without Activation, a plan is just a dream, not the reality you and others experience.

ACTIVATION INVOLVES STRETCHING INTO LIVING YOUR

AUTHENTIC SELF IN EVERYTHING YOU DO.

STRETCH INTO YOUR POWER ZONE

I am going to say it straight. Almost all of us are in our comfort zone doing work that isn't on purpose and isn't in our highest impact and highest value areas – our power zone. Audiences almost everywhere will eventually agree with me – after the initial shock and partial denial. We are living in our comfort zone... not our power zone.

There are four zones, as shown in Figure 3:

- Comfort zone

- Stretch zone

- Fear zone

- Power zone

POWER ZONE THINKING

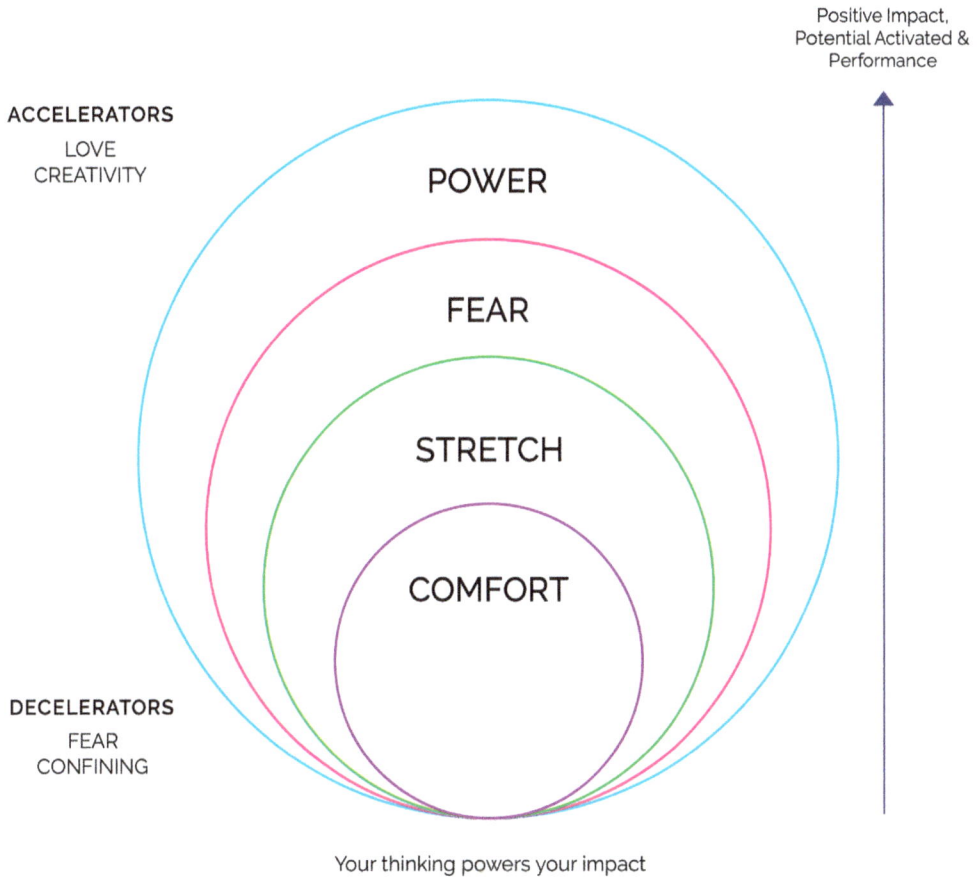

ACCELERATORS
LOVE
CREATIVITY

Positive Impact,
Potential Activated &
Performance

POWER

FEAR

STRETCH

COMFORT

DECELERATORS
FEAR
CONFINING

Your thinking powers your impact

Figure 3: 4 Zones

© Kellie Tomney

Comfort Zone

Your comfort zone means you are not growing. You are doing the same or similar stuff that you did last year, or (more of a concern) that you've done for many years. You go through the motions; you know how to do it almost on autopilot and it's a fairly common occurrence. You could do this type of work all day every day and not challenge yourself at all. You are behaving as though this is easy and you may question the value of what you are doing. To move out of your comfort zone and into your power zone, you focus on your purpose and higher impact and value priorities. You need to *purposefully* stretch.

Common comfort-zone examples are your everyday role, your expertise and your easy, repetitious tasks, meetings and relationships.

FUTUREPROOFING ACTIONS

Reflect on the following questions:

- What is in your comfort zone?

- What percentage of your working week do you spend in here?

Stretch Zone

Your stretch zone means you are stretching to grow. You are doing some new stuff or doing some things differently. You are feeling a little nervous as you are trying new things for you. You are not on autopilot. You can feel like you're at a new gym class – the moves aren't as seamless, you aren't familiar with what's next and you can feel 'new' muscles after it, some you didn't know you had! You know it's working and it's making a change, and you are inspired to keep going to new classes when you feel you are getting comfortable and fewer results again. You are embracing new skills and approaches and changing your behaviour accordingly. It can be difficult at first;

you often need some new strategies and support (that personal trainer and coach can be invaluable, giving you new techniques, making modifications that make it more impactful and cheering you on). To move up out of your stretch zone, you focus on your purpose and keep stretching and progressing into your power zone.

Common stretch-zone examples are: important meetings, presentations, interviews, public speaking, branding and promoting yourself, social media, sales, networking, influencing senior stakeholders and/or important clients, difficult conversations, performance reviews, asking for a pay rise, going for a new job, applying for a new role and having career conversations.

Great individuals and leaders, and their teams and organisations, live in the stretch and power zones. When you live in these zones – and make the effort in this stretch zone – the universe delivers at an accelerated pace. Take positive steps by completing stretch-zone actions towards your purpose. Watch as your pay rises and you gain more interesting roles, more responsibility, promotions and more influence; watch as your contribution accelerates and amplifies. Experiment with stepping further into your next stretch-zone actions and you will notice your inner power unlock. You will become more and more impactful.

FUTUREPROOFING ACTIONS

Reflect on the following questions:

- What is in your stretch zone?

- What percentage of your working week do you spend in here?

- Look back at your Limitless Vision & Goal Cast and Career Purpose – what are the highest value and impact actions needed to achieve them? Hint: They are probably in the common stretch-zone examples above.

- What are the THREE stretch-zone actions that will make the biggest difference to you now for your future? (For many, it's branding and promoting themselves, applying for new roles and having career conversations.) They are often the ones you talk yourself out of doing!

Fear Zone

Your fear zone means you are nearing your power zone. You are stretching into high-impact and high-value priorities and you are growing. You can feel like you want to stop and go back to your easy comfort zone. Your mind chatter and self-talk can get loud and be constant. You are behaving a bit erratically here; you can second guess yourself and you can be talked into wanting to go back into your comfort zone, being 'smaller' and working on things that are less significant. The fear-zone layer can be thick. The thickness can pull you back or you can master techniques for it to propel you forward into your power zone. To move out and up, you witness your fears, you acknowledge what is helpful and what isn't, and you proceed with stepping forward into your power zone.

Common fear-zone examples are fearful thoughts such as:

'I am not experienced enough. I need an MBA.' I don't know how many times I've heard this one. Not one organisation has said to me, 'We need someone with an MBA.' Not one. In the top twenty CEOs globally, eleven don't have an MBA (HBR). Let alone those who take an entrepreneurial path; many don't have university qualifications. Qualifications ALONE don't put you in the power zone.

'I'll go for it when the kids go to school / when my boss leaves, etc.'

'I don't want the organisation to find out.'

'I really love my team; I couldn't do it to them.' Loyalty, even if it is authentic and deep-rooted, is a delayer.

'I am not as good as...' Comparisonitis.

These fears keep you small.

Our most common fears are: fear of failure, fear of standing out from the crowd, fear of success, fear of conflict, fear of not being liked, fear of being judged, fear of losing relationships and the holy grail of fears... the fear of not being good enough.

It's important to note that your fears won't vanish. Your fears can protect you. Fears can get thicker and faster and louder when you are coming into your stretch and power zone.

This is ground-breaking work. I definitely recommend working with someone on this. Ideally someone who is going to help you to face your fears with compassion, let go of your limits and help you through to your power zone.

Procrastinator, perfectionist, avoider, denier, delayer. I've been all of these at different times in my career and none of them have helped. Forgive your fears and ego-based thoughts and, most of all, yourself for thinking them. It's human but it doesn't have to limit your positive impact.

The fear-zone barrier before our power zone can seem impenetrable. I remember reading Brené Brown's book *The Gifts of Imperfection* ten years ago and it changed my life. It contains powerful and profound research. It reveals scientifically that we all experience fear! It's not just you or me – we all experience it!

'If we want to know why we're all so afraid to let our true selves be seen and known, we have to understand the power of shame and fear. If we can't stand up to the *never good enough* and *who do you think you are?* we can't move forward…' says Brené.

I see this every day with every client, male or female, irrespective of age, race or education, etc. When we get real with ourselves, fear is in all of us.

> *Nothing holds you back more than your fears.*

Typically, we avoid discomfort at all costs, without realising the total opportunity cost, and the opportunity cost is huge!

You are good enough. Notice when the fears come up – accept they're there for most of us. Your judgemental inner critic will be saying, 'What will others think?' 'I am not perfect at this yet,' 'I am too old,' 'I am too young.' Just know that you are good enough and step into an empowering thought and action that will help you achieve your purpose and vision.

Sometimes, just noting the stretches down can bring up the fears. Fear can rule our lives and hold us back, whether we are conscious of it or not. But once you've noted your fears, you can focus on the stretch Activations to get into your power zone.

I've lost count of the number of women in particular who fall prey to 'I'm not good enough' and so won't apply for the next job. Recently, a client found out another person was applying for the role she wanted so she was losing sleep about whether to apply or not. She really, really wanted to work for this company. Thankfully, her husband said, 'Speak to Kellie.' We worked through the job description (which we know is a wish list) and she was more than capable for the role. In truth, she then realised the role wasn't such a stretch for her – she could add more to it! She stepped through her fears and we prepared her and she applied feeling far more confident. At the time of writing, final interviews are in progress and she's been told she in the top two for two roles. What is most significant is her growth in confidence, power and soon to be impact. The company she's wanted to work for for years is disrupting and innovating a whole industry with national impact and she is going to be in her power zone to deliver the benefits to customers.

FUTUREPROOFING ACTIONS

Reflect on the following questions:

- What is in your fear zone at present and for your Limitless Vision & Goal Cast?

- What percentage of your working week do you spend in here?

'YOU NEVER CHANGE YOUR LIFE UNTIL YOU STEP OUT OF YOUR COMFORT ZONE; CHANGE BEGINS AT THE END OF YOUR COMFORT ZONE.'

– ROY T. BENNETT

Power Zone

Your power zone means you are in your own personal power. You feel empowered. You feel on purpose. You are in your talents and truth, and you inspire and help others to be the same. You empower not overpower. You are moved by your purpose and you create and influence movement in others. Your potential is activated. Your performance is high and getting higher and your positive impact is expanding and being amplified.

You are living your Career Purpose, you are undertaking high-impact and high-value stretch-zone actions but now with more presence, influence and authentic power. It radiates from you. You are behaving in your career, work, meetings, presentations, discussions and all relationships in a powerful and consistent way aligned with your purpose, your brand and the future you want to create. You have your core and you adapt to different contexts for improved impact. You behave like it's what you were born to be doing and being. You relish being in your power zone and it's accelerated your career and influence. You know your four zones at present and you actively ensure you are always adding some stretch to keep expanding your power zone for increased positive impact.

An example of being in your power zone can be giving a presentation and feeling you've truly connected with the audience, getting spontaneous feedback about how you've understood their problem and helped them figure out the solution. Perhaps you're working across industry sectors on key economic and social issues, such as more sustainability, more manufacturing in Australia, more renewable energy for the future. Perhaps you're being asked to co-found environmental collaborations, etc. It's authentic to you, it's future-aligned and you've stretched and developed yourself to feel in your authentic power zone doing this work. It's in your internal and external brand; it's the experience others have with you. It's in every touchpoint for you – online or offline. It's in everything you do. It's who you are, who you want to be and what you love contributing in the world.

TAKE YOUR POWER BACK.

FUTUREPROOF YOU

KELLIETOMNEY.COM

Many people feel powerless rather than powerful. Many people come to realise they have given their power away. You must own your power. You need to make your most purposeful positive impact. To do this, you acknowledge your fears, and you claim and activate your power.

You stretch into your power zone with the clarity of your future vision and the courage to step through your fears to activate more powerful outcomes and make your unique contribution.

You need to put in the effort to move past your comfort zone. The rewards are on the other side of your stretch.

Over time, your stretch zone becomes your comfort zone. That way you are always growing. The magic happens in your power zone.

FUTUREPROOFING ACTIONS

Reflect on the following questions:

- What is in your power zone at present and for your Limitless Vision & Goal Cast and Career Purpose?

- What percentage of your week is spent here?

- What or who can help you consistently step into and stretch through to your power zone?

- What do you want to be in your power zone?

PUTTING IT INTO PRACTICE

Commonly, clients say they are living in their comfort zone. Even though the hours or stress can be high, they are not using or stretching into using any new future-valued skills. I've had the chief operating officer of a major global financial company realise she was ninety-eight per cent in her comfort zone! There is no judgement – just realise where you are and where you want to be.

So, what do people want in their power zones, I hear you ask? For many, it's being authentically powerful in their stretch-zone actions, e.g. powerful presentations, powerful meetings, impactful conversations, powerful impact, powerful influence, powerful presence, impactful interviews.

Here are some of my personal examples to help:

- Comfort Zone: Organisational leadership programs. 1:1 personal brand mentoring and workshops.
- Stretch Zone: Focused, dedicated book writing.
- Fear Zone: 'You should be getting onto other work.' 'You can't do this.' 'It's too big.' 'Others aren't doing it.'
- Power Zone: Global online group workshops. Speaking. Completing this book and becoming an author.

As you can see, it's not helpful staying in your comfort zone. The stretch may be a little uncomfortable, but it's what propels you forward. While you may not love doing some of the stretch actions (many can't stand public speaking!), the fear will become less. The stretch-zone actions will get you to your power zone so you can achieve your purpose and vision and goals!

Choices, moment by moment, change your life. So, always choose a stretch action to progress to your future-aligned power zone.

Key stretch-zone Activations from my clients are included later in this chapter. Review which ones stand out for you. For many clients, it's about starting on the internal work first and then turning to the external. Check in with yourself and figure out where you are now.

Activation builds your internal character and your external career and impact.

We don't grow in our comfort zones. We grow from our power zones.

To stretch into your power zone, activate your highest value priorities every day – things you are working on internally and externally.

Think of Activation like brand activation for a business. A common example is Coca-Cola. The business ensures every touchpoint a person has with Coca-Cola is as consistent as possible. The exact red, the excitement in the advertising, the exact flavour.

Coca-Cola can charge a premium (and does) because millions globally know, like and trust the brand, it's message to them and its delivery.

Say you love a brand in store but when you have to order online you have a terrible experience. The value of that brand to you is lessened. You may not buy from them again; you may tell your friends; you may go on social media and complain online. The value goes down.

So, like a business or product brand, I've applied these principles to personal branding – to people like you. Like any brand, we do business and create careers with people whom we know, like and trust (whether we are conscious of it or not).

CONSISTENT BRAND ACTIVATION THROUGHOUT ALL TOUCHPOINTS DELIVERS

EXTRAORDINARY VALUE AND INCREASED IMPACT.

AUTHENTIC ACTIVATION – INTERNAL

When it comes to careers, there are many touchpoints; you are with people every day. Unfortunately, it's not as easy for people to be as consistent as a Coca-Cola recipe that hasn't changed since invention in 1892.

I've broken the highest impact Activations for your career into two groups. The first Activations are to do with your thoughts. I've grouped them as Authentic Activation – Internal:

- Actively and consciously aligning and living your brand.

- Mastering your mind.

- Creating career opportunities.

- Futureproofing your highest value and impact in your days, weeks, months and years.

- Personal adaption to constant and emergent change.

Let's activate these critical, internal touchpoints for maximising your career.

Your thinking powers your impact. It either accelerates you towards the future you want or decelerates you, keeping that future distant.

The brain learns with repetition and rehearsal. We think over 60,000 thoughts a day on a ninety-second loop.

Neuroscientific research shows the effect that your thinking can have on your life. If you set the intention on your brand, purpose and vision every day, it will have a remarkable, positive impact. Your thoughts become your reality. They are who you are internally and externally.

'Stress' has been dubbed the 'health epidemic of the 21st century' by the World Health Organization and is estimated to cost American businesses up to $300 billion a year. (WHO, 2016) Career and leadership cause a lot of stress; they have a huge impact on your life. Managing the modern mind clutter and the 'always on' mentality often limits us from making our biggest impact.

Meditation and mindfulness are like a personal trainer for your mind. Your mind is like a muscle; you have to exercise it. Mastering your mind increases your clarity, confidence and ability to be present and at your best. I recommend increasing your awareness and trying different ways to meditate and be mindful. One of the most powerful ways to raise your vibration is to master your thoughts. It is a major secret weapon when it comes to futureproofing you to reach your career and life goals.

I teach modern meditation and 5Ms: Meditation, Manifestation, Mindfulness, Mantra and Music. Many clients use this in their daily practice and have transformed to be the best they can be in their career and leadership choices. They have become a better friend / partner / wife / mother / aunt / husband / father, etc. Your thoughts are the soundtrack you listen to all day long; they are helping you make a bigger or smaller impact. You can choose a different soundtrack to help you transcend the noise of daily life.

Every day, you are planting seeds for your future reality.

Which thoughts will help you now for your future?

FUTUREPROOFING ACTIONS

Reflect on the following questions:

- Are you **actively and consciously aligning and living your brand** and who you want to be in everything you do?

- Are you **mastering your mind** for your highest impact?

- Do you **create opportunities** to build your brand and positive impact for the future?

- Are you **futureproofing your highest value and impact in your days, weeks, months and years**? Are you **closing the gap** between what you want your future to be and what you are doing day to day? Are you establishing **helpful boundaries and expectations**?

- Are you able to **adapt, pivot and be present** and of highest value no matter what change, challenge or celebration comes in?

AUTHENTIC ACTIVATION – EXTERNAL

Have you ever been told how wonderful an organisation is to work for in an interview touchpoint and then gotten to the end of the first month only to think, 'Is this the same organisation?' Was it not what was promised? Not what was expected? There are big consequences for the organisation and so too for individuals. If you are consistently high value and high impact and what you say and promise are authentic, consistent and valued, then what others see, experience and feel in all their interactions with you is aligned and leveraged.

These are the Activations that others see, experience and feel. I've grouped them as Authentic Activation – External. These are more to do with how you present yourself in person and online – all day every day. Remember, we are on 24/7. People are googling you in preparation for their meetings, interviews, etc. and they're doing it when it works for them (that could be online at midnight in another country).

I know most of you hate activating branding… that's because you are not doing it authentically and it's making you feel small and insignificant! Once you do it authentically, I know you will come to actually love it. It's true!

I've given here the highest impact, highest value Activations to future-proof you to achieve your future vision and goals:

- LinkedIn (you are googled before people go to a meeting – know this)
- Your new world CV/resume
- Brand presence, image and style
- Personal brand impressions and impacts
- Powerful meetings
- Impactful career conversations
- Impactful interviews and 'casual' career conversations
- Powerful presentations
- Impactful network and networking

If you know, look and feel authentically confident, you will perform and authentically present confidently. You control how you act, how you are perceived and your impact.

Which of these will help you now for your future?

FUTUREPROOFING ACTIONS

Reflect on the following questions:

- Does your **LinkedIn** present your authentic self for your future-aligned vision and goals?

- Do you have a new world **CV/resume** that presents your best self for your future-aligned goals? Does your value stand out in a six-second read?

- Do you **feel, look and live your brand** in everything you do? Inside and outside of work so you feel yourself, fulfilled and whole?

- What are the **personal brand impressions and impacts** people have of you today versus in the future?

- Do you add the value you know you can in **meetings**?

- Have you been having **impactful career conversations** to make your career goals and aspirations known to key influencers in your organisation and externally?

- Are you prepared to give your best in **interviews and 'casual' career conversations**?

- Can you give **powerful presentations** on the positive impact you are making in your career?

- Are you **networked** in the areas you want your future career and impact to be in? Is it helping you create your future and adding value to connections also?

ACTIVATE YOUR CAREER & IMPACT

In Activation, I encourage you to be at your highest impact, highest value always. I have clients who are achieving more in their career, working fewer hours and having stronger relationships, health and growth because they are aware and they choose 'highest impact, highest value'. That means the lowest value, lowest impact work may not get done, and guess what, no one misses it. When others see your highest value and highest impact, they know what you can contribute and that's where you play and are powerful. That's the new level for your career and impact.

Step into being more.

If you are doing things or focusing on things that you don't value, you are literally devaluing your life and impact. Any time you take an action that is aligned with your highest purpose, vision and brand, you amplify that action and impact. You shine and the positive impact expands. You show up with purpose, power and an aligned, trusted brand and identity; you are consistent and connected to your passion, career and future.

Any time you step back or shy away from your purpose, your vision or your views, you reduce your value. Any time you step forward towards your purpose, your vision and your views, you increase your value. Importantly, this is both to yourself and to others.

If you don't activate your highest impact, your potential is wasted, your impact is diminished and you don't feel valued; you feel you are one of many and you can feel lost and like a fraud or imposter, unfulfilled and purposeless.

It matters because we need your views; we respect people who speak up. You can't just keep your head down and get picked for promotion – it won't happen. You'll always be overlooked for someone offering authenticity, uniqueness, value and a higher impact.

There is increased competition for jobs, for projects, for board roles, for community leadership… you may be good, but you've got to be the one. You have to step in and show up. They want an outstanding person and you have to activate that internally and externally to make your aspiration your reality. Your purpose and brand give you power and connect your future to your current reality and the new world we are in now.

So, take a moment to ask yourself some honest questions:

FUTUREPROOFING ACTIONS

Reflect on the following questions:

- What are your highest impact and highest value priorities from your stretch and power zones to achieve your Limitless Vision & Goal Cast?

- What are your highest impact and highest value priorities from the Authentic Activation – Internal list?

- What are your highest impact and highest value priorities from the Authentic Activation – External list?

- Looking at your answers, are you spending and investing your time, energy and efforts on these?

'IF YOU DON'T PRIORITISE YOUR LIFE, SOMEONE ELSE WILL.'

– GREG MCKEOWN

POWER ZONE PRIDE

Like lions, our leadership, clarity, confidence, courage, power and contribution inspire others into their greatest impact and futureproofing for all.

Own your power to self-author and self-transform. Too many of us succumb to losing or surrendering control of our own career and lives. So many of us get lost and don't know how to take control of our own path and how to elevate ourselves and our impact.

The combination of Authenticity, Alignment and Activation for amplification of your positive impact and growth will help you to take control and keep you focused and inspired to keep activating.

When you have these keys working in your unique, valued combination and in harmony, you are truly you, your future vision and most valued abilities are becoming reality, and you're activating in your power zone. You become abundant and super-powered! This is where you truly attract incredible opportunities and you amplify the impact you were born to make. You do your life's best work.

YOU ARE PURPOSE DRIVEN. YOU ARE VALUES DRIVEN.

YOUR ACTIONS AMPLIFY YOUR UNIQUE, AUTHENTIC IMPACT.

KEY POINTS

You are a result of your choices and actions.

◆

To maximise your career and impact, you must stretch into your power zone. Nothing grows in your comfort zone, except previous career stories and highlights!

◆

To create your best career contribution yet, you step through your fears to action high-value stretch actions every day. It becomes who you are. You enjoy the challenge, the mastery, the increased impact, and it pulls you forward into your power zone.

◆

In Activation, I've applied brand and marketing principles to people and careers. Product and service brands that are consistent in every touchpoint are more highly valued and make much more impact. It works for people and careers too!

◆

There are crucial Internal Activations and External Activations.

◆

Know your highest value Activations and improve them in order to meet the new world.

◆

Activate your biggest impact every day.

ACTIVATING YOUR POWER ZONE

Sabrina was clear on where she wanted to go in her career. She was a manager in the FMCG sector. She loved the organisation she worked for and she had a goal role but she realised she wasn't optimising her potential and performance. She had heard me speak at a Women in Leadership Conference on Authentic Personal Branding and knew that she wanted to do something about it. She wasn't maximising her personal brand and she didn't know what to do to get to her career goal role.

We worked together through the 'Futureproof You' framework. The Authenticity key gave her clarity, Alignment balanced her work and life goals, and she was onto Activation quickly. We prepared her for maximising meetings and presentations, interviews, powerful career conversations and building her ideal week and clear ninety days in advance – all living her Futureproof Personal Brand.

She was promoted in three months. When she asked why she was promoted, her business leaders replied, 'You are much more confident. You are speaking up and you've really stepped up.' She was clearer in her views and spoke up more powerfully and authentically. It paid off for her personally and professionally.

We worked together on her next level of activation priorities, addressing what was in her comfort zone, what was a stretch for her to reach her goal, and the fears that came up when she tried to do the new important things.

It became clear there were only four things that would really power her forward to meet her goals (that gave her confidence in itself!). I coached her through targeted, strategic career and performance review conversations. Her next level of activation priorities became: influencing senior stakeholders, next level negotiations, and more team management to show and develop her leadership even further. She got the next role and was recognised across her whole business; she was seen as a role model internally and externally in her work and life.

Once she realised what she needed to stretch through and activated more of those high-impact actions, behaviours and beliefs, she accessed and was activating her power zone. Having been promoted internally within three months of working together and soon after achieving another promotion, she stretched again and exceeded every key performance indicator. She achieved a 'no backing needed' performance appraisal with all stakeholders excited about her career trajectory in future.

What do you need to do to stretch out of your comfort zone into your power zone?

Part 3:

AN EVOLVING ADVENTURE

Being yourself and having a future-aligned plan is not enough. Futureproofing is constant and consistent – it never stops. It's not a set and forget activity.

There is no final destination, as I used to wish! You are where you are and you make the best of it using these keys every single day.

You continue to unlock new levels of Authenticity, Alignment and Activation. You step further into your unique superpowers, living your values, creating and living your future now and activating new, enhanced ways to make your biggest, best, most fulfilling impact.

Living your Career Purpose and making an important impact at higher levels pulls you further into your power and along the path.

This is our human and soul journey to be more fully who we are, to share our superpowers and to continually grow.

To maximise your career and life, an adventure mindset works best. Pack your purpose, your creativity, your curiosity and all your best supplies and skills. You are the central character. You create and choose in your career and life adventure. Like all good adventures or stories, you will be challenged to grow into who you truly are and all you can be. The cycle of impact fuels you on and the development path is your treasure map.

Your career and life really can be much more fun, more fulfilling and more financially sustaining than they currently are... believe me!

So, let's keep going.

A CYCLE OF
IMPACT

I have a client called Sandra whom I've worked with since meeting her in 2017. She has experienced so much change. Her business was expected to maximise its growth for sale. Having been Head of Customer Operations, and having shown real talent with people and numbers, she was given the Head of People & Operations role. This grew to include all of finance as well. The business was then approached for sale. They had to merge with another business and she got the Head of Integration role, bringing the businesses together. With the head office moved to another state that wasn't really sustainable longer term for the next stage of the business, the impacts of economic change and industry disruption hit. Sandra was offered redundancy or roles that didn't stretch her. She has now been approached by a private equity investor to prepare a business for further growth. They've seen her stretch into really adding value to a business through their people, culture, operations and financials. But she has other options also.

This is just some of the change she's experienced. She's needed to constantly evolve because of the increased pace of change.

Her challenges have been many and varied:

- Keeping up with and leading the business through the upheaval, change and disruption;
- Keeping herself and her family at their best throughout the many challenges;
- Keeping and improving engagement and connection across different sites;
- Working from home;
- Legislative change that affected the business model and sustainability of the businesses; and the list goes on.

All the while, we worked to consistently focus on where she wanted to go and whom she was growing into being, maximising the impact for all parties.

> *Ever-growing involves continually evolving to live your purpose for your highest impact contribution today and in our new, better future.*

'THE ONLY CONSTANT IN LIFE IS CHANGE.'

– HERACLITUS

DON'T STOP GROWING

According to career change statistics, the average person will change careers five to seven times during their working life. With an ever-increasing number of career choices, thirty per cent of the workforce will now change careers or jobs every twelve months.

The rate of change and complexity is increasing. Post 2020, it's sped up even further. We haven't been here before.

There are said to be three choices that exist in life: giving up, giving in or giving it all you've got. I'll be giving it all I've got and I want you to join me. I'll be ever-growing, continually learning, and adapting to the future and new reality, with its further disruptions, opportunities, complexities, capabilities and careers, seeking the highest good for us globally and locally.

Often, the start of a new phase of growth and of evolution is epitomised by a test or challenge. It can be a tragedy or trauma, but most often it's an everyday test.

I've experienced a point where my career and life path were nowhere near where I'd expected them to be. After three years, I collapsed under the weight of it all. I couldn't see a way through, nor any light at the end of the tunnel. I am shocked and devastated to say that I got to the point where ending my life seemed to be the only way to put an end to my lack of purpose, potential and impact being realised. I couldn't see another path forward for my future and what came next. Thankfully, my connection to something bigger (and this methodology) saved my life and livelihood. This is the reason I am here today sharing this career- and life-empowering process with you!

Your transformation is unique to you – it doesn't have to be a tragedy or trauma that sparks it. Proactive pivots are recommended! Notice the career and life obstacles early and ever-grow.

'OBSTACLES ARE DETOURS IN THE RIGHT DIRECTION.'

— GABRIELLE BERNSTEIN

FUTUREPROOF YOU

KELLIETOMNEY.COM

Like the process of a caterpillar becoming a butterfly, we are supposed to evolve and grow.

Ever-growing allows you to continually unlock your next level of amplification and expansion of impact and value.

> *Your career and life will have inevitable ups and downs. If you are in greater Authenticity, Alignment and Activation, you will have much more purpose and peace and far less pain.*

'WE DELIGHT IN THE BEAUTY OF THE BUTTERFLY, BUT RARELY ADMIT

THE CHANGES IT HAS GONE THROUGH TO ACHIEVE THAT BEAUTY.'

– MAYA ANGELOU

REFRESH AND EVOLVE

So, how do we continue to evolve?

There is a continuous cycle for growth and continuing to increase and amplify your career and impact. There are sustainable actions that you need to be aware of, as shown in Figure 4.

It important to understand where you are on this adventure and when you need to move to the next stage or do a comprehensive new loop!

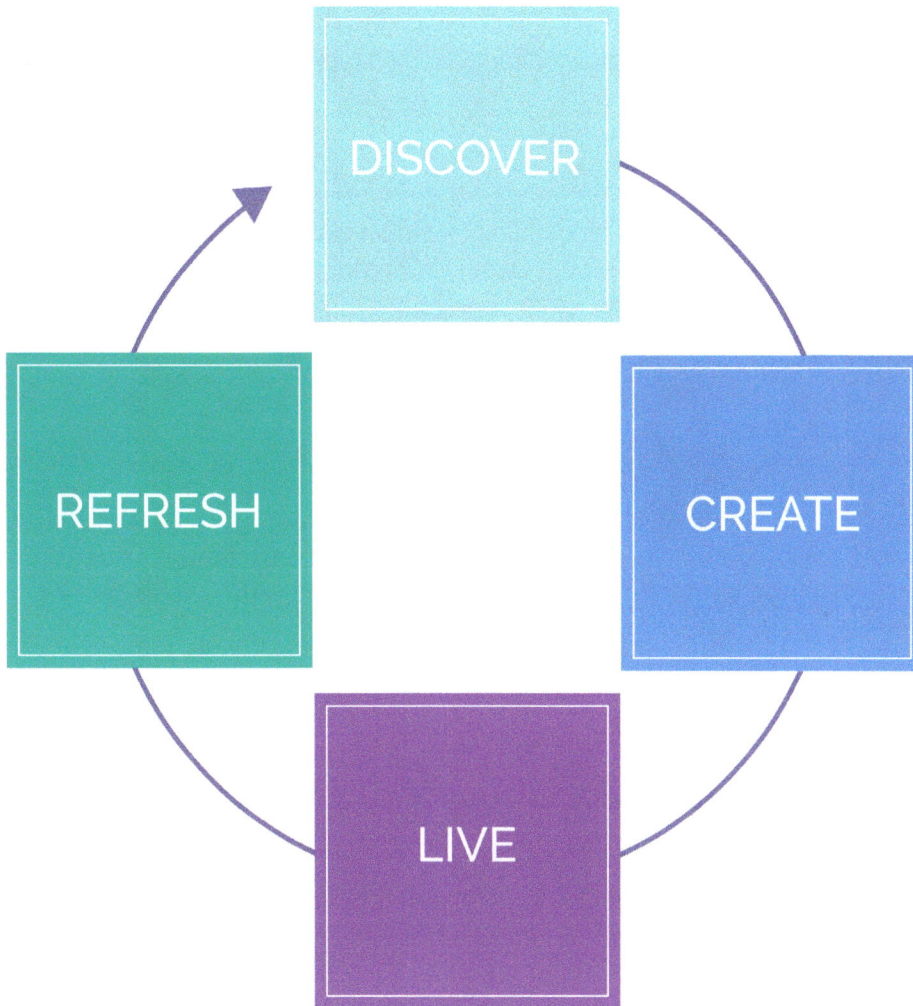

Figure 4: Evolving Cycle

© Kellie Tomney

Discover

This really helps when you feel you have outgrown your current situation or you sense that you need to be proactive regarding 'what's next' again. At this stage, you connect with who you really are at this point in your career and life. Don't ignore the call, your instincts and/or external changes. Discover!

Create

This comes when you have clarity from Discovery and you want to employ strategic, purposeful tools aligned with your future. In Create, you develop your future plan, your futureproof brand and the career combinations that fit your life and maximise the impact you want to make.

Live

This is when you are really putting your authentic future into practice. In the Live stage, you are activating your authentic self and are consistently maximising your brand. You are focusing on the highest value priorities for the greatest impact. You are stepping in and relishing who you are and the increasing impact you are making.

Refresh

At the Refresh stage, you've either noticed you've started to stall or you've experienced an external catalyst for change (commonly job, organisation, industry, health or relationship change) or an internal call for more growth and the opportunity for greater impact. You either want, or have been pulled into, your next level of growth. In Refresh, you capture all the learnings you've garnered to get where you are today, and you complete another cycle at a new level for you.

It's likely through this book you've started Discover and Create! It's great, no doubt, getting more clarity from Discover and more confidence from Create, but without stepping into Living your brand and biggest impact and Refreshing your contribution... well, it isn't as valuable. Genuine futureproofing is the entire cycle. The true, long-term benefits are in these four stages of growth. They help you really change gears in your career and life!

EVER-GROWTH IS AT THE HEART OF A FUTUREPROOF PERSON.

They never stop.

They thrive on it.

They have learned to fully appreciate where they are now and they have future-valued direction and a healthy hunger for amplifying their positive impact in their 'what's next'.

THE STAGES OF ADULT DEVELOPMENT

Now we're here, I'll also share a treasure map unknown to many. There are stages of adult development, with plateaus and transition points along the way. It is useful and heartening to know this, especially when you meet one on this adventure. It's good to know that you are not alone (as we can so often feel). You must acknowledge that there can be serious pressure points in your career and life and you can lose your way.

What's more, it's a good thing. While I know it is challenging if you are in a transition, in the future, we need more people who are able to deal with increased complexity. Conditioning is so powerful at keeping us the same, in the familiar, but the best adventurers move forward into the unfamiliar, where you get to create the best adventure for your career and life.

These transitions and developments mark some of the most difficult *and* most joyous and rewarding times in my life. With your brand as your North Star, these stages can show you a pathway forward.

I've simplified and adapted the Stages of Adult Development here, as shown in Figure 5. To explore them in further detail, please go to kellietomney.com.

FUTUREPROOF DEVELOPMENT STAGES

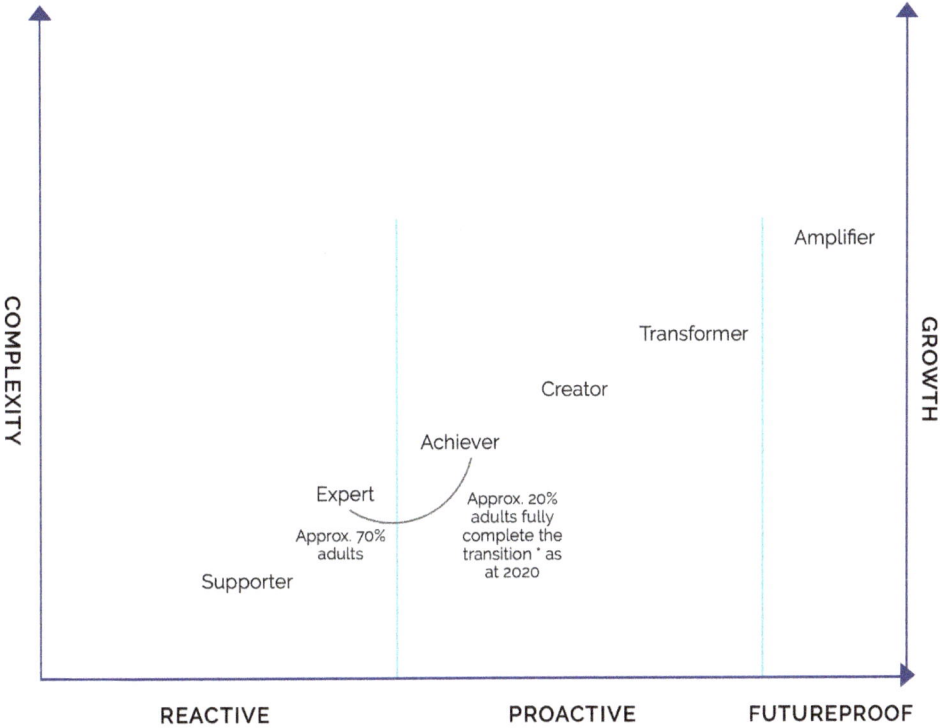

COMPLEXITY

GROWTH

Amplifier

Transformer

Creator

Achiever

Expert

Approx. 70% adults

Approx. 20% adults fully complete the transition * as at 2020

Supporter

REACTIVE

PROACTIVE

FUTUREPROOF

FUTUREPROOF DEVELOPMENT

Simplified & Adapted from Dr. Edward J. Kelly 2014, Stages of Adult Development

Figure 5: Futureproof Development Stages

© Kellie Tomney

Most adults are reacting to their current environment, with approximately seventy per cent in the early stages of development. To get ahead of the current environment, we need more people in the Proactive stages of their career and life. Approximately only twenty per cent fully complete the transition to become more proactive, creating their own career and life adventure. When you are Futureproof, you are ahead of any environment. My aim is to get more to this point, where people are leading, amplifying and helping others to grow amongst the increased complexity of the future, with more of the world's population futureproofed in their careers and lives.

It is my belief and experience that we have more professionals in transition than ever before. Transition challenges who you really are, what your identity is, and your relationship with work and life changes. There is a pathway from 'I am my job,' to 'I can create my career (and life),' to 'It's us creating our careers and world.'

In transitions, you can feel like you don't fit the mould; you've outgrown your job and/or organisation and are pulled towards 'what's next'. The 'Futureproof You' framework helps you on this path to creating your career and life.

There are going to be more free agents, more portfolio careers, more 'Brand You, Inc.', more global entrepreneurs and intrapreneurs, more leaders, and more self-trading professionals, where the boss is you, the service and skills are you, and you need to brand and sell yourself. I know because I'm working with them. And no matter where they are on the development path, they know they are on a path of growth so they can manage through higher complexities. They recognise they may either be in a stalling plateau, a growth spurt, a transition or a major transformation.

They continually choose, moment by moment, change by change, Authenticity, Alignment and Activation as their keys. Their career, value and impact just keep amplifying further and further. Challenges appear but they are clearer, stronger and more adaptable, able to move forward confidently and positively.

This ever-growing approach allows you to embrace and adapt to change, transition and transformation *while* staying true to your authentic core and purpose. It allows you to lead yourself and others through change with bravery, vulnerability, courage and realistic optimism. Your character, ethics and integrity are intact and building trust *and* you are adding new, valued skills to new levels and outcomes for your organisation, leadership, career, life and planet. You keep, at your core, evolving your career, your calling, your growth and skills, *and* your impact and life.

> *Doing this 'Refresh review' ensures you stop running from your true calling and live your highest value and most positive impact on the planet.*

FUTUREPROOFING ACTIONS

Reflect on the following questions:

- Discover: Where are you in the Futureproof Development Stages currently and where do you want to be next? What is your current personal brand reality for this point of your career and life? (Refer back to the chapters: From Frustrated to Futureproof and Key 1 – Authenticity)

- Create: What is your next career and future plan? What multiple, valued career combinations and options meet this plan? What does your next Futureproof Personal Brand need to be for your next future-aligned plan? (Refer back to Key 2 – Alignment)

- Live: How do you activate your next highest value priorities to live for your aligned future? (Refer back to Key 3 - Activation)

- Refresh: What has changed (internally and externally) and what do you need to retire, reimagine, refresh, reset, add and update to make your next highest impact?

'I NOW KNOW WHO I AM.

I am more than a wife and mother. While I love these things, I can be myself. I am myself. I know what I am worth and I am valuing who I am. I brand how I represent myself everywhere: in life, at school, on my committees, industry council, etc. I am bigger and better and I am going to smash it. I want to keep this up and superpower my time every month and on the next level – especially before my next job. I feel futureproofed. I have options. I have finances. I am independent. I have great friends and little kids. I am in my power zone.'

Amy, Health, Safety & Environment Manager, proud mum

GROW TOGETHER NOW

We all have so much to gain by living and sharing our unique, most positive super-powers in careers, leadership and life.

I've seen clients:

- Discover their career, leadership and life purpose.

- Leverage their time and focus on their most expensive asset (with a 100 per cent success rate).

- Align, activate and amplify towards growth by forty per cent.

- Unlock fifty to ninety-five per cent extra potential in themselves and existing people in their team and organisation.

- Unlock authentic, confident, empowering, ever-growing leaders, talent and pipeline.

You will evolve. You will grow evermore into who you authentically are and into your purpose and your gifts. You will be aligned and in your joy, serving the world and yourself.

'THAT'S WHEN WE'RE AT OUR BEST,

WHEN WE SUPPORT EACH OTHER.

NOT WHEN WE CANCEL EACH OTHER OUT FOR PAST MISTAKES, BUT WHEN WE HELP EACH OTHER TO GROW, WHEN WE EDUCATE EACH OTHER, WHEN WE GUIDE EACH OTHER.'

— JOAQUINN PHOENIX

FUTUREPROOFING ACTIONS

Reflect on the following questions:

- What is your next level of amplification and expansion?

- What is your next most positive impact in the Future of Work and your life?

- Who are the next leaders you can encourage and amplify?

- What is your next level leadership legacy and big impact?

- What is your next level contribution to the world?

'IN OUR RESPONSE LIES OUR GROWTH AND OUR FREEDOM.'

– VICTOR E. FRANKL

FUTUREPROOF YOU

KELLIETOMNEY.COM

KEY POINTS

Changes and challenges will continue. No one is immune.

◆

Ever-growing involves continually evolving to live
your purpose for your highest impact contribution
today and in our new, better future.

◆

Implementing the Cycle of Impact: Discover, Create, Live and
Refresh ensures your career and you remain futureproof.

◆

You are not alone if you feel you've outgrown your current
career and are looking for more fulfillment and purpose.
It often means you are ready for the next level!

◆

Through this cycle, you keep contributing more with less stress.

◆

You become the person contributing
what you were born to impact.

EVER-GROWING IMPACT

Kathy, a previous client, contacted me. She wanted to take her career development to the next level. She was on a career track in her current organisation and it had been taken over by a larger organisation. She didn't know the leaders and influencers in the new organisation. She felt her brand, at its core, hadn't changed, but her circumstances and context had completely changed. She wanted support to maximise her next 'what's next'.

She had enjoyed the benefits, the increased impact and influence and balance, from our previous work a couple of years prior and now she wanted to prepare and position for this next organisation. Internally, she wanted to prepare for the next stage and next level of impact. She didn't know how to keep her core and reprogram and reposition for this next level.

There was an even greater opportunity to expand her influence and impact and grow her career.

We had previously worked through Discover, Create and Live and she was now ready for the next level. In honest reflection, she had now gotten back to being in her comfort zone; she could stretch more and the new change provided even more opportunity for her in her power zone. We did a review and Refresh and discovered that we could authentically stretch her brand further now. We developed her next new career and future vision (whole of life), we realigned her priorities, and she now lives her intentions for the future and has the flexibility and options to be fluid with the future as it comes. She had new challenges with increased competition for next-level roles. We prepared for powerful career conversations, next-level, external and internal branding, and got even more focused on her futureproofing, non-negotiable, high-impact and high-value priorities and the negotiations and courage to stick to them.

She has grown to the next level. She has more abundant and growing career options, her salary and value have increased, and her relationships with her clients and new and previous colleagues are now richer. She is amplified in her influence and impact. More people know of her, her skills and value, she is at the table for key meetings and she is continuing to rise to her next level of impact. She is navigating increased complexity with greater impact.

Like a circle, the cycle is completely whole as it is. It allows you to stand in the circle – own your power, inside and then out. The ever-growing cycle allows you to expand that circle and your impact to be bigger and bigger. She is feeling even more her 'full self', she is making more impact, she is making more money, and she has more balance, less stress, more mindfulness and stronger relationships.

She is making the next-level contribution only she can make and she is enjoying the career combination she wants for this stage in her career and life.

Like Kathy, your future is what you create.

So, what will you go and do?

CONCLUSION

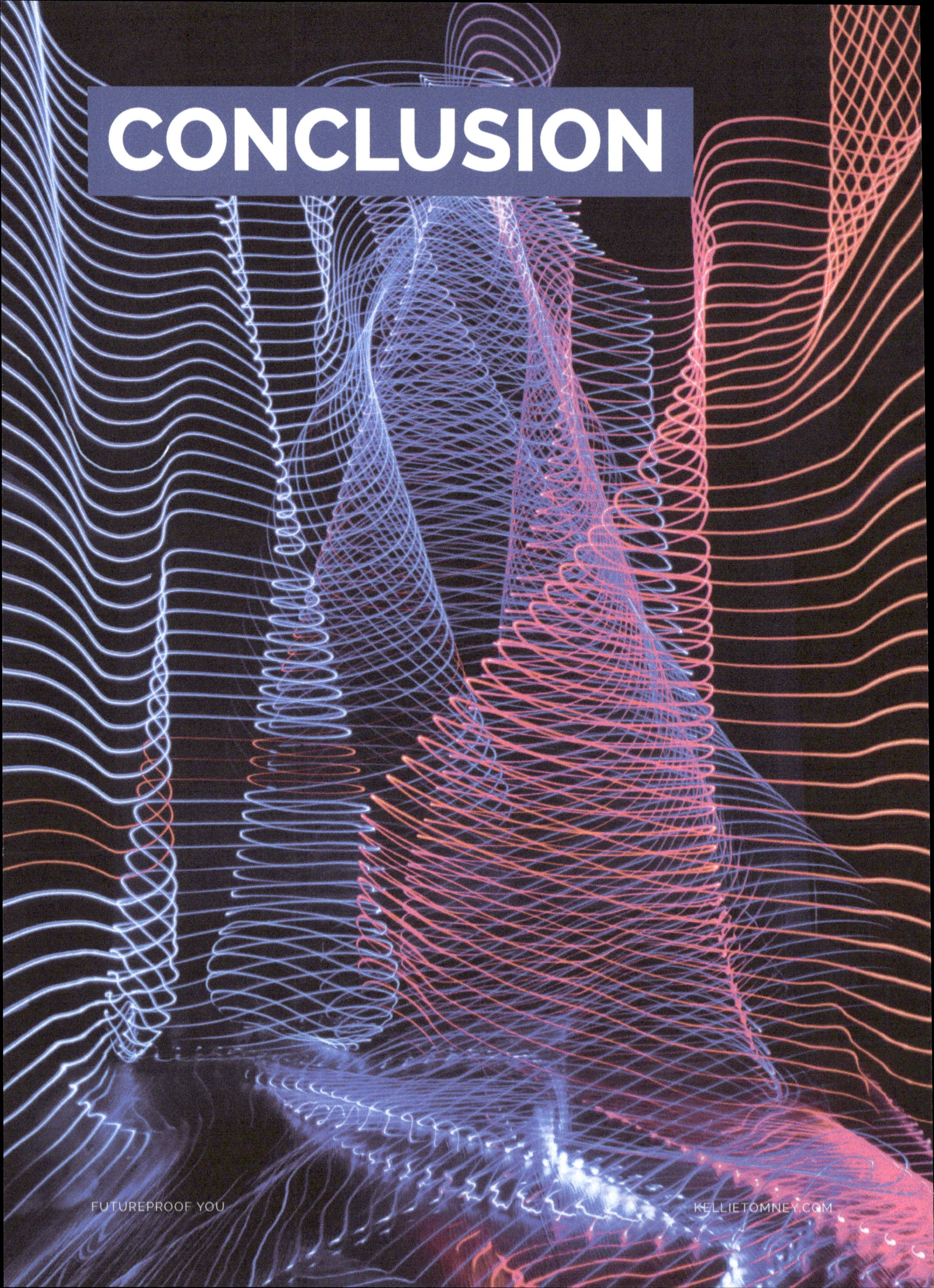

Let's finish with a question.

- Why were you drawn to this book in the first place?
- Do you feel you can make more of an impact in your career? In your leadership? In your organisation? In your industry? In the world?
- Do you want to work out 'what's next?' for you?
- Do you feel like you'll regret it if you don't prepare and position for the ever-changing future now?
- Do you struggle with bringing your best, whole self to your career and work?
- Do you really do yourself justice with your personal branding? Especially when it comes to maximising those high-value performance appraisals, career conversations, pay discussions, critical meetings, job interviews and speaking opportunities?
- Do you want to set yourself up with authentic collateral to ensure you meet your career goals? Do you think your LinkedIn, CV/resume, meeting style, etc. might be out of date and not reflective of you and your value and the new world of work?
- Are you a humble achiever, fixer and/or doer who wants to add more value, expand and create an even better future?

Yes?

Well, I hope, by now, you realise that you absolutely can bring your whole self to your career and work. You have unique superpowers that you can share with the world for far more impact. You are good enough; everyone has fears, but you have to step into authentically branding yourself to be considered and amplified in the Future of Work. Competition is high for existing jobs and new jobs will be created requiring skills you may not have yet. You can purposefully create your future. You can purposefully choose the path. You can be on the exciting new adventure ahead. Being in your authentic core *and* being adaptable.

So many executives and professionals have their career progression stalled and feel stuck. You can be unlocked. You can define your Career Purpose, connect with your power, create your identity and connect to your passion in your career and organisation and industry.

You can be prepared and positioned for career and future change. You can turn the worry and overwhelm about 'what's next' into clarity, confidence, courage and greater contribution. You don't have to be frustrated in your career. You can have more fulfillment than you have experienced. I have clients with the evidence.

All you have to do now is the purposeful work!

Remember your 3 Futureproofing Keys:

Authenticity:
Get clear on you, your superpowers, your differentiators and values: your STANDOUT ADVantage.

Alignment:
Develop your future and career plan, your unique futureproof brand, and options and value that build your confidence and contribution.

Activation:
Action the highest value touchpoints so you can be your brand in everything you do. Take action with authenticity and alignment to amplify your positive impact. Stretch into your power zone.

What's more, remember it's an Evolving Cycle of Impact. You continue to adapt and grow. You remain amplified, alive and valued into the ever-changing future.

There is so much more than this book.

I know you are busy and I wanted to give you the Futureproofing Keys concisely so you can get to purposefully actioning the words and work here, versus a brick of a book that you just sit on the shelf and never get to.

So, now it's up to you.

I invite you to trust the inner voice that drew you to this book.

We need you.

We need your unique superpowers.

We need your authentic, whole best.

We need you fulfilled in your career.

We need your purposeful contribution.

We need you in your power zone.

We need you to *be* it so we can see it.

You can *be more.*

You can *create a career and life you love.*

You can *impact so much more.*

Yes, you can.

Let's do this!

KELLIE TOMNEY
authentic fulfilled limitless.

YOUR FUTUREPROOF REPORT AND RECOMMENDATIONS

Do you want to find out HOW
FUTUREPROOF you are right now?

To find out your Futureproof level, go to:

www.kellietomney.com

Take the free FUTUREPROOF YOU indicator
quiz and receive a personalised report and initial
recommendations to get you moving forward

CONNECT WITH ME

I still remember somehow getting hold of a copy of the story of The Body Shop founder, Anita Roddick, as a teenager (*Body & Soul: Profits With Principles*). It opened up my whole world, a world away on a farm, population of five. A book can change a life – your life. So thank you for taking the time to read mine. I encourage you to please gift and share this with others you think it could help.

My purpose is to amplify the positive impact of as many people as possible in my lifetime. If I can assist you, please get in touch on one of the below channels.

Let me help you and/or your company futureproof and make a bigger, more positive impact. I would love to bring this to reality.

My most positive impact contribution is through speaking, workshops and mentoring (online and in person). Key topic areas are:

- The Future of Work
- Futureproofing Careers
- Leadership & Organisations
- Change & Transformation
- Personal & Leadership Branding
- Women in Leadership
- Meditation, Mindfulness & Mastering your Mind
- Purpose, Resilience, Impact, Innovation & Performance.

If you want expert guidance and support to futureproof you, your career, your leaders, your talent and/or your organisation, contact me to assist with:

- Actively building your organisation, leadership or career for the future
- Actively finding solutions and activating growth
- Unlocking the hidden value of your executive leaders and talent
- Embracing and activating the Future of Work
- Growing your pipeline of talent and capabilities for the future

- Growing your organisation, career, impact and soul
- Leading and living purposefully and powerfully
- Making your most positive impact

I have online and in-person programs on:

- FUTUREPROOFING YOU
- RESETTING YOU
- 1:1 & Group Coaching, Mentoring, Executive Coaching & Facilitating Groups
- FUTUREPROOFING ACTIVATORS

Ways to connect and get in touch:

kellietomney.com: Subscribe to my e-news and you will receive authentic career and leadership stories and *Coffee with Kellie* videos, strategies and tips to inspire and keep you ahead in leadership and career impact.

Email: kellie@kellietomney.com

Phone: +61 432 085 708

I'd love you to connect with me on social, as the futureproofing evolution continues for us all! I share live videos, Q&As and encourage connection and sharing success stories and inspiring support to help you. To get your book bonuses, go to kellietomney.com.

Follow and leverage the latest on:

- kellietomney
- kellietomneyfutureproofing
- kellietomney
- kellietomney
  #futureproofyou

ARE YOU READY TO FUTUREPROOF

AND MAKE YOUR MOST POSITIVE IMPACT?

Let's do this!

Remember, futureproofing is an adventure.
And I've love to connect with you on yours
to make it the best possible!

Meantime, my best,

Kellie

K x

SOURCES

THE PROBLEM WITH BEING PASSIVE

AI driving the start of a 'unique' technological era, IBM Chief Executive and Chairman, Ginni Rometty, March 2018, Australian Financial Review.

FROM FRUSTRATED TO FUTUREPROOF

Career Fulfillment Survey Diagnostic, 2020, Kellie Tomney, hosted on kellietomney.com

KEY 1: AUTHENTICITY

10 Brand stories from Tim Lebrecht's Ted Talk, Kate Torgovnick, May, TED Blog, 2012. https://blog.ted.com/10-brand-stories-from-tim-leberechts-tedtalk/

Women who run with the wolves, Clarissa Pinkola Estes, Ph.D, 1992.

KEY 2: ALIGNMENT

A New Earth: Awakening to Your Life's Purpose, Eckhart Tolle, 2008.

Careers 3.0 Future Skills Future Work, Time spent on Career Planning, Workforce 2020 skills, Dr. Tracey Wilen-Daugenti, Apollo Research Institute. https://www.oecd.org/site/eduimhe12/Tracey%20Wilen-Daugenti.pdf

AI will change 100% of the jobs over the next decade, IBM Chief Executive and Chairman, Ginni Rometty, CNBC, 2019. https://www.cnbc.com/2019/04/02/ibm-ceo-ginni-romettys-solution-to-closing-the-skills-gap-in-america.html

More control over careers breeds more engagement and innovation and reduces stress, *The Infinite Game*, Simon Sinek, 2019.

What Is Employee Engagement and How Do You Improve It? Gallup, 2020. https://www.gallup.com/workplace/285674/improve-employee-engagement-workplace.aspx

Future Work Skills 2020, Institute for the Future for the University of Phoenix Research Institute, 2011.

https://www.iftf.org/uploads/media/SR-1382A_UPRI_future_work_skills_sm.pdf

KEY 3: ACTIVATION

THE CEO 100 - 2019 Edition, Harvard Business Review, 2019. https://hbr.org/2019/11/the-ceo-100-2019-edition

The Gifts of Imperfection, Let go of who you think you're supposed to be and embrace who you are, Brené Brown, 2010.

Workplace Stress: The Health Epidemic of the 21st Century, Huffington Post, 2016.

https://www.huffpost.com/entry/workplace-stress-the-heal_b_8923678

A CYCLE OF IMPACT

Obstacles are detours in the right direction, The Universe has your back, Gabrielle Bernstein, 2016.

A Developmental Autobiography: Plateaus and Transitions in My Development as an Adult includes Adult Development Path, Integral Leadership Review, Dr. Edward J. Kelly, 2014. http://integralleadershipreview.com/11732-article-3-developmental-autobiography-plateaus-transitions-development-adult/

The Hero with a thousand faces, Joseph Campbell, first published 1949.

Stages of Development, Spirit of Leadership, Bob Anderson, 1998. https://executivemandala.com.au/resources/

CONNECT WITH ME

Body and Soul: Profits With Principles: The Amazing Success Story of Anita Roddick & the Body Shop, Anita Roddick, 1991.

ACKNOWLEDGEMENTS

I knew from a young age that I wanted to make my biggest impact. What I learnt very quickly is that you can't do it alone.

The great Isaac Newton said, *'If I have seen further it is by standing on the shoulders of Giants.'* I stand on the shoulders of the Giants before me who have put their thought leadership out in the world to benefit others. To each and every one of them, and my mentors, I thank you.

I want to thank the many leaders over my career, in particular Gordon Cairns, Nicolette Wood and Karen Lonergan (I know I will wish I added more here), and the organisations (there are too many to mention) and the communities, such as Employer Brand International, HR Awards, Business Chicks, Telstra Business Awards, Women in Leadership, Women in Focus, Women in Banking & Finance, Ruby Connection, Future Women, Women's Agenda, Thrive Global and Thought Leaders Business School, that have inspired me to keep on my purpose and continue in the belief that we can do work differently (and better) and we can always improve the future.

To the expert support crew (each in their superpowers!) who have helped me create a book that I know is authentic, aligned and activated for the impact I want to make in the world. Kelly Irving (master editor – for expertly helping me get what could have been seven books down to one!) and the Grammar Factory Team (Scott, Sara, Jake, Julia and Dania). You've made it as powerful as I envisioned it to be, thank you. There will be more books to come.

To my constant support and loves:

To my husband Garie, for your love, challenge and care on our adventure with our common purpose of maxing our superpowers, careers, lives and legacy for good.

To my Mum and Dad, who didn't have the career options available to us today, who encouraged me to live 'the world is your oyster' from a farm in remote South Australia and taught me to always strive for excellence.

To my friends, for their continued support as I persistently pursue this life-long purpose of 'what's next' in the future, focusing on how we improve it and max our fun and fulfillment along the way!

I am truly deeply thankful for all above, the ocean, and my meditation and Bondi communities.

To each and every one of my clients – Individuals, Leaders and Organisations – you inspire me every day. There are too many to have in one book and I look forward to celebrating your growth and impact on Coffees with Kellie and in the books to come!

To you – I needed this book, so I wrote it for you.

I've travelled the realm of commercial business and emotional, financial, mental, physical and spiritual dimensions to create this framework. So, thank you for reading and starting your 'what's next' Futureproofing adventure with me.

My intent is to inspire and amplify your positive impact. Be your best, most impactful self and take action with purpose!

K

ABOUT THE AUTHOR

Kellie helps senior leaders, own bosses and executives propel forward, transform their careers and amplify their impact in the future of work.

Putting you on the fast track to achieving your career dreams and unlocking EVER-GROWING executives, leaders, professionals and organisations isn't just a career for Kellie – it's her calling.

She can help you futureproof your career, leadership and organisation. She's fixated on adding the fulfillment, financial sustainability and fun in our careers and lives. (We've lost our way on this, haven't we?!)

After building an award-winning corporate career in Branding, HR, Leadership & Transformation, Kellie founded her own consulting business during a challenging period – personally, professionally and globally. Having learnt powerful and life-changing lessons, and having experience of many different career models (professionally and personally), she embraces the challenges and the strengths of corporate, entrepreneurial and free-agent mindsets to build careers of the future.

Kellie was the first woman in Australia to successfully implement Employer Branding in organisations. She was also the first woman to bring Personal Branding to leaders and corporate women. Having sat on HR awards judging panels for over ten years, she continues to review and work with companies to improve their leadership and positioning as Employers of Choice for women and diversity, dedicating her efforts to empowering women and leaders, equipping companies to diversify their management teams, and amplifying their personal and leadership brands. This said, she is most proud of her clients who have proactively created the careers and lives they have dreamt of.

Kellie is recognised world-wide as an expert in emerging fields. She is now a highly-sought-after online and in-person career coach, speaker and mentor on Personal & Leadership Branding, Women in Leadership, Future of Work, Careers, Embracing Change and Increasing Resilience & Adaptability, engaging with various industries including Professional Services, Banking & Finance, FMCG, Government, Tech and Energy. As a many times nominated Telstra Business Woman of the Year, Kellie is recognised as achieving market-leading results for individuals and businesses.

She has worked with and created powerful outcomes for a wide range of executives, professionals, free agents, own bosses, business founders and company clients, including: Woolworths Group, Origin Energy, KPMG, Apple, LinkedIn, Westpac Group, Commonwealth Bank, St. George Bank, Quantium, Louis Vuitton Moët Hennessy (LVMH), Unilever, Campbell Arnott's, Coffey International, Plan International, Unisys, Gartner, NSW Health, Transport for NSW and The Corporate Executive Board.

She encourages you to own your future and think and amplify BIG, positive impact. She thrives on a great morning coffee, meditation, the beach, great people, great music, fun and creating our best Future of Work and world.

kellietomney.com

KELLIE TOMNEY
authentic fulfilled limitless.

TESTIMONIALS

'**If ever there was a time to take stock and invest in yourself, the 2020 decade is it!** As we all navigate seismic shifts in our work and home lives, it is great to have Kellie Tomney on our team, challenging us to achieve our career potential and enhance every aspect of our lives along the way.'

BELINDA BIBLE, CHIEF OPERATING OFFICER

'**Kellie's ability to help me unlock and activate my whole self has given me the power to manifest exactly what I want in my career and life.** She truly has the ability to listen, see the bigger picture and inspire you to think differently. I have also learned from Kellie that my personal growth is never complete, and I cannot thank her enough for continuing to help me realise my true potential.'

AMANDA CONEYWORTH, DIRECTOR & REGISTERED LIQUIDATOR, KPMG RESTRUCTURING SERVICES FOUNDER OF GORGEOUS PRESENCE

'Kellie is smart, savvy and talented with a distinctive humility and grace about her character that sets her apart from others. It is powerful to experience Kellie's goddess-like energy in person – extraordinary intuition and empathy that paves the way for deep connection. This is where Kellie is in her element and works her magic. **If you seek to uncover hidden female talent in your organisation and develop leaders that truly make a difference, look no further.** Kellie's ability to identify and unlock hidden potential in people, so that they operate from a place of autonomy, strength, and abundance, is truly transformational.'

STEPHEN SCOTT JOHNSON, INTERNATIONAL MENTOR, AUTHOR OF *EMERGENT – IGNITE PURPOSE, TRANSFORM CULTURE, MAKE CHANGE STICK*

'Many of us have the drive and willpower to achieve goals, but sometimes we are so busy 'doing' the goals when they come about that we fail to see how much more limitless, futureproofed and fulfilling our careers and life can be and what we could aspire to with just a little more support.

When realisation struck for me that having 'everything' – my own business, board positions – was still leaving me unchallenged, unfulfilled and entirely disengaged, the astute feedback, challenge and mentoring that Kellie Tomney provided helped guide me back to find the core things that I loved (my superpowers!) and focussed me on doing those things in a whole new way.

Two years on, **I enjoy a growing, successful business, an even greater team, doing the work I love. Proof having a mentor, a person in your corner, like Kellie Tomney, can make your goals limitless and you truly fulfilled.**

I am thankful to have her in my professional and personal tribe. I'd recommend her being in yours.'

MOYA STEELE, PRINCIPAL, KEIR STEELE WALDON LAWYERS

www.ingramcontent.com/pod-product-compliance
Lightning Source LLC
Chambersburg PA
CBHW052337210326
41597CB00031B/5288